Growin' Up Good

A humorous, common sense blueprint for raising your child to become a responsible, thoughtful, happy person.

By Dr. Norma Campbell

Ballast... It's all about ballast.

Webster's New Collegiate Dictionary:
ballast: Something that gives stability, esp. in character and conduct.

GATEWAY PRESS, INC.
Baltimore, MD 2004

Copyright © 2004 by
Dr. Norma Campbell
All rights reserved.

Permission to reproduce in any form
must be secured from the author.

Please direct all correspondence and book orders to:
Norbel School
6135 Old Washington Rd.
Elkridge, MD 21075

www.norbelschool.org

Library of Congress Control Number 2004102016
ISBN 0-9749985-0-8

Published for the author by
Gateway Press, Inc.
1001 N. Calvert Street
Baltimore, MD 21202-3897

www.Gatewaypress.com

Printed in the United States of America

This book is dedicated to the memories of both my wise grandmother, who often told me when I was upset... that, unless I killed someone... anything else is fixable, and my mother, who taught me the profound understanding of 'So What!'

Contents

Contents

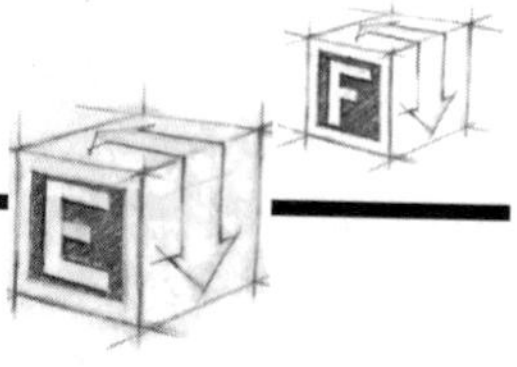

ACKNOWLEDGMENTS

More than three decades ago, as a newly licensed psychologist, I attended a lecture by the eminent Dr. Albert Ellis. From that first encounter, and many to follow, his profound conception and development of REBT strongly influenced both my personal life and the lives of countless clients throughout my professional career. REBT has provided the tenets from which many chapters of this book have derived. Thank you, Dr. Albert Ellis.

I acknowledge the help afforded me by John Winokur in his book, *The Portable Curmudgeon*. From it came many of the famous quotes that enabled me to maintain a humorous presentation in my attempt to teach the principles of good parenting.

Introduction

GROWIN' UP GOOD

... We are given children to test us and make us more spiritual.
... George Will

Do you remember that old story about the three religious philosophers who endlessly debated such ponderous matters as the true beginning of life? The first young leader concluded that life begins at birth, while the second insisted that life begins at conception, not birth. "Which of us is correct?" they beseeched the third, older sage. The wise philosopher smiled. "Neither," he replied, "for it is clear to me that life begins only when the last child moves out and the family dog dies."

For sure, sages have long contemplated why reasonable adults ever choose to have children. The mere topic of child-rearing has provided the grist for many a curmudgeon to sharpen his tongue and gleefully ride forth in battle against that terrible affliction called 'parenthood.' Adhering to the well known strategy that to be forewarned is to be forearmed, these witty humorists, whom I call 'witics,' have long tried to prepare us. Sam Butler, an early curmudgeon, observed that, "some people seem compelled by unkind fate to parental servitude for life" and concluded, "there is no form of penal servitude worse than this." Peter Devries warned, "The value of marriage is not that adults produce children, but that children produce adults."And then there is Martin Mull, a modern 'witic' who may have presented the same message best, less elegantly perhaps, but crystal clear. He wrote, "Having a family is like having a bowling alley installed in your brain."

Finally, no less than Bill Cosby, that quintessential comedic parent, questioned what makes people ever want to raise a child, and even he could only conclude that people have babies because they make decisions by the heart and not the brain. Cosby figured that raising a kid to 'grow up good' is about as likely as hitting the daily double. I believe he might be correct because emotional reasoning, in reality, is tantamount to little or no reasoning at all. That is, making decisions by the heart and not the brain may just be a polite way of saying that people make a lot of dumb choices... and that certainly pertains to child raising. Hence the need for this book.

Most parents are well intentioned. Unfortunately, good intentions are inadequate to ensure that a child will 'grow up good,' because we all know that old saw about paving roads with good intentions... you see, creating a baby and raising a baby are mostly opposites. One is easy, requires little effort, happens quickly and provides pleasure. That's the creating part. The raising part is something else. It involves hard work and patience, is often tedious, frustrating and not always pleasurable. You might say parenting is one of those deals that has GOOD NEWS and BAD NEWS attached to the fine print. Here's the GOOD NEWS first. You really can beat those daily double odds! And even better, all you need are some simple guidelines to follow, which have been burned into your brain and will pop out automatically no matter what the situation. Think of it something like what athletes call 'muscle memory.' Well-trained athletes with muscle memory will avoid most problems to begin with, but when they do encounter a glitch in their system, they can diagnose the dilemma quickly and renew their muscle memory. This same principle applies to parenting. You will not be an expert automatically when you have created a child. Hardly. But just a few simple nuggets of knowledge can make parenting pleasurable and successful much of the time, while you are waiting for your child to grow up and move out and that family dog to die. That's the GOOD NEWS. Now for the BAD NEWS. While parenting guidelines are simple, simple is not the same as easy. Just as in developing muscle memory, converting 'simple' into 'easy' requires practice. Understanding is important, of course, but understanding, alone, is not sufficient. And you might as well hear the rest of the BAD NEWS; parenting has no room for wimps! Not only must you be willing to practice, you must be persistent and brave. I once heard of a book called *Parenting Is Not For Cowards*. I may not have read it all but I sure liked that title.

Every child expert agrees that a wise parent will stay in charge of the child, no matter if the child doth protest. That truism seems so clear. Why, then, is it not easy? Staying firm is not easy because, remember, well intentioned parents respond to feelings and not to logic. You want your child to be happy and you hate to disappoint him. He is adorable and irresistible. Your angel appears to be vulnerable and helpless, and in many respects he is. You feel responsible and you worry a lot. What you don't recognize as readily is that babies are not only helpless and vulnerable, they are totally unsocialized.

Introduction

Mother Nature made a few goofs in her timing, it seems to me, because babies stay unsocial much longer than they remain helpless. You see, babies get smart quickly... not about everything, but how to get their way. Babies get smart quickly, but parents smarten up to that fact slowly. So the stage is set for the baby bandit to take control. The tables turn and you become the victim of your baby. And it happens as quick as a wink!

About this book. I guess you might say that this book is about common sense, common sense in helping your child 'grow up good.' We can't take common sense for granted, particularly in child raising, because, to review, we now realize that new parents are not experienced in the wily ways of young children, we smarten up slowly and we continue to make parenting decisions by that same emotional reasoning that brought us to parenting in the first place. Worse yet, even when we manage to think logically, often we don't follow through with sensible action. Anatole France said it well... "It is human to think wisely and act foolishly." Now you don't need a Ph.D. to raise a child into a happy, good person. In fact, many psychologists may have messed up everybody with too many theories and too much psychobabble.

Over the years, parents have often referred to my bits of practical advice as NORMA'S NUGGETS. You will find them scattered throughout the book, sort of like bottom-liners. So here's **NUGGET #1**:

BABIES GET SMART FASTER THAN YOU THINK.

Try to remember that.

The contents of this book will provide you with the simple ABC's of 'GROWIN' UP GOOD.' You most likely are wondering just what I mean by that title. To me, 'growin' up good' means a child grows gradually and steadily in his ability to own responsibility for himself; how he thinks, how he feels and how he acts. An adult person who has 'grown up good' understands that he is not perfect nor is anyone else, either... so he doesn't take himself too seriously and can laugh at the absurdities of our humanness. That makes him an understanding, forgiving and loving person. He pursues his wants in life with gusto, without collapse when he runs into those inevitable hassles, and when they occur, he can discipline his disappointments and move on, reasonably. That makes him the captain of his emotional ship, not its victim. A child who is 'growin' up good' feels happy in a contented, peaceful way most of the time and he has developed a set of values which reasonable people admire. You will like your child, others will like him, and most important, he will like himself. What else would you really want for your child?

Chapter A

ABOUT THOSE ANGELS—
Alex, Ashley and Andy

"... A child is a curly, dimpled lunatic."
... Ralph Emerson

First things first! You can't help your child to 'grow up good' until you understand the nature of your angel. Just what is your child all about, anyway? What makes him tick and what do you really need to know about parenting him? In the old days, long before unisex, the answer to 'what is a child?' was clear. Everybody knew that little boys were made of toads and snails and puppy dog tails, while little girls were made of sugar and spice and everything nice. Well, now we have become more sophisticated and we understand that those descriptions simply will not do. Besides, those who have lived with seven year old girls probably have suspected that little boys were getting a bum rap. So, in the spirit of truth as well as equal rights, if boys are toads 'n snails and puppy dog tails, then girls might better be described as whines 'n wails and tattley tales... that sounds a bit more fair, wouldn't you agree?

We recognize that kids come with more equipment than tails and wails. In fact, your angels are born with an incredible repertoire of skills. Your angel has highly efficient lungs, abundant energy and curiosity, wonderful observational and memory capabilities... but most important, perhaps, is your angel's immeasurable capacity to be cunning. At first, cunning-adorable, then soon, cunning-adorable combined with cunning-crafty. Cunning is such an important ingredient in your angel that it has warranted a chapter devoted exclusively to it... CHAPTER B: BABIES KNOW THEIR BUSINESS!

If you already have consulted a medical expert, you may think you know all the vital parts of Alex, Ashley or Andy. Probably you have educated yourself about proper vitamins and inoculations, about strong teeth and healthy blood. You certainly know something about their G.I. system, the gastrointestinal one, and how best to keep your baby's tummy comfortable. But do you know anything about your angel's OTHER G.I. system, the secret one..the powerful one that dictates his behavior, his motivation, his will and gradually the building of his character? Do you know THAT one? Well, if the experts neglected to describe his second G.I. system, let me introduce you.

From the moment of conception, what do you think your angel is doing all that time in the dark? He isn't sitting there doing nothing. He is busy. Your angel is preparing for the grand inauguration of his motivational program, and at birth or shortly thereafter, it will be launched. Motivation, you see, is merely a fancy word to describe how people use their energy chasing what they want in life, namely PLEASURE. Try to envision a motivational system comprised of two magical potions, the G.I.s—The G's and the I's stand for GIMMEEs and IDONWANNAs. The GIMMEEs are the positive potions because they are busy chasing positive pleasures. At first, all positive pleasures are GIMMEEs... GIMMEE food and drink...

GIMMEE hugs and smiles... GIMMEE toys to make me laugh and have fun, and then, as if that isn't enough, pretty soon the greedy little beggars add on the LEMMEEs. LEMMEE wiggle... LEMMEE see it... LEMMEE have that... LEMMEE do it myself!

GIMMEEs and LEMMEEs make up the positive motivational program I call the TRIPLE M: MAKE MY MOMENT! GIMMEEs and LEMMEEs are your angel's authoritarian command to you: "MAKE MY MOMENT, AND DO IT NOW!" All the while Alex and Ashley have you hopping, attending to their GIMMEEs and LEMMEEs, they have their other magical potions working also... the IDONWANNAs. IDONWANNAs are considered negative pleasures because they are aimed to keep your angel from feeling pain or discomfort. That is, negative pleasures result from escape-and-avoid motivators. IDONWANNAs make up the motivational command I call the DOUBLE D: DIMINISH MY DISCOMFORT! Negative pleasures are experienced as relief, a very good feeling to your little angels, who find ways to tell us about their IDONWANNAs. IDONWANNA feel cold or hungry or have a tummy ache... IDONWANNA be bossed or controlled... IDONWANNA sit still if I feel like wiggling... IDONWANNA listen to you or obey you or feel hampered while I am chasing my GIMMEEs and LEMMEEs. IDONWANNA wait even one minute for my pleasure, either... if you try to interrupt my magical juices I will roar as loud as my lusty lungs will allow, until you DIMINISH MY DISCOMFORT and MAKE MY MOMENT once again.

The relentless pursuit of pleasure is found in all people, not just children. Everyone wants to experience pleasure in some form, as often as possible, at the least cost possible and to hold it as long as possible. Seeking positive pleasure is natural and healthy and is the 'human way' to be, a truism separate from issues of morality. This you need to understand and accept in helping your child 'grow up good.' Negative IDONWANNAs are natural and healthy too, most of the time, as long as they stay in reasonable balance with GIMMEEs and LEMMEEs and don't take over the whole motivational system. That seems easy to understand but not so easy to control! And, as Alex and Ashley grow older, their IDONWANNAs become more sophisticated and subtle. That is, what kids consider painful is no longer merely bodily discomfort. These additional IDONWANNAs include... IDONWANNA feel stupid or foolish... IDONWANNA feel lonely or helpless... IDONWANNA be controlled, bossed or tricked.

When positive GIMMEEs and LEMMEEs directly compete with negative DIMINISH MY DISCOMFORT the DD usually wins. I believe it to be the more powerful motivator. In a conflict most people will choose to avoid or escape pain rather than pursue positive pleasures. And the experience of immediate relief from discomfort is so powerful that pursuing the DD can predominate and habituate quickly. These IDONWANNAs, if allowed to run rampant, do not allow your angels to 'grow up good' because too much time and energy, spent trying to guarantee that they won't feel uncomfortable, will keep Alex, Ashley or Andy from trying new experiences that would provide positive pleasures. Just such an unfortunate program describes what happens to people who become depressed and fearful. They don't maintain enough positive GIMMEEs and LEMMEEs in their life because they are afraid to run risks.

Just one more unfortunate note about pleasures. I have designated a third category which I call PERVERSE

PLEASURES... They are not part of a normal, healthy motivational system and should they predominate, would guarantee to prevent children from 'growin' up good.' Perverse pleasures become motivators only if your angel cannot successfully experience enough appropriate GIMMEEs and LEMMEEs and IDONWANNAs. If Alex, Ashley or Andy experience pain over and again without recourse to successfully avoid or escape discomfort or failure, they gradually begin to feel pleasured in being cruel or by teasing other people in hurtful ways. They might feel good by overpowering other people, controlling and forcing them to cry "Uncle." Bullying behaviors and taking revenge are examples of PERVERSE PLEASURES, as are stubborn power-struggles. I truly believe such perverse motivators are symptomatic of children who are not 'growin' up good.' ..sort of like a glitch in the motivational system that requires fixing.

New parents need to recognize, of course, that since all young children are unmindful of the wants of others, often they will run over somebody's rights in their natural pursuit of GIMMEEs and LEMMEEs. Such is the nature of a child's Triple M: MAKE MY MOMENT, not to be confused with a perverse pleasure.

In many important ways babies and grown people are alike. We are all precious just because we are human. We all have GIMMEEs, LEMMEEs and IDONWANNAs which drive our motivational systems. Above all, no one wants to feel bad... not babies and not grown people. We all have feelings, and we respond to them most of the time. We all want to be 'connected' and to communicate to others how we feel. These are some ways that children and adults are alike. But there exist important differences between your little angels and you, which need to be understood if you are to help them 'grow up good.'

Children have been wrongly defined over the last century, prompting misconceptions and causing parents to be misguided in their attempts to raise their angels. At the turn of the 20th century children were thought to be miniature adults, rather like tiny people, albeit with weak musculature. Their brains were believed to be already fully developed at birth and thus young children were expected rather early to be trained to think logically, with adult reasoning processes. We now know that to be untrue. Young children cannot think complexly; even into adolescence frontal lobes are still developing. Their thinking is concrete and absolutistic, 100% black-or-white, all-or-nothing. Alex and Ashley do not understand the concept of the passing of time for many years because they cannot grasp abstract concepts. That is why your young angel is so often not ready for school on time, and dawdles while you wait impatiently, no matter how you scold! Young children cannot enjoy the humor of a play-on-words, because they think only literally, not figuratively. I remember, one time, confronting my 5-year-old son Billy with his hand in the proverbial cookie jar. I said, "Aha! Caught you red-handed," and to my amusement, Billy pulled out his hand and examined his palm carefully. His all-or-none reasoning was evident on another occasion when our family dog chewed a new shoe. Said I, in exasperation, "Oh, look at this: now what will we do with this dog?" Billy replied with great solemnity, his eyes as big as saucers, "I guess we will have to kill him."

Children simply cannot handle a complex chain of logic required in making an observation, evaluating the outcome, drawing a conclusion and finally abstracting a generalization, using a variety of relevant cues... come to think of it, not too many adults get that far either! It all boils down to this... children are not miniature adults. It takes a very long time for Alex, Ashley or Andy to handle abstract concepts.

Something else children are not, as infants, toddlers and even preschoolers... they are not socialized in that they are 100% self-centered. They have little or no ability to share, to empathize, to play fair, to be careful about another person's feelings, to be appreciative, because they have no concept of "otherness." Your angel's every concern and interest is "ME" centered. Such is not evil, but merely the human way to be in the early years. Much like thinking skills, developing a sense of otherness and a grasp of the reciprocity principle of 'you and me together' takes a very long time, and requires modeling and guided practice.

So Alex, Ashley and Andy are not miniature adults. They are not abstract thinkers and they are not socialized. And you might as well acknowledge one more in this list of 'are nots'... perhaps the most critical: young children are not patient. Not only are they unable to think complexly, they feel in the same 'all-or-none' style as they think. Unlike adults who have many shades and degrees in intensity of feelings, children seem to have but two. Your angels are 100% happy or 100% miserable and they move from one feeling state to the other about as fast as a jackrabbit jumps. Alex, Ashley and Andy want their GIMMEEs, LEMMEEs and IDONWANNAs and they want them NOW! That is the foundation for their positive MAKE-MY-MOMENT and negative DIMINISH-MY-DISCOMFORT motivational system.

In fact, children's pleasure pursuits differ dramatically from adults'... that is, those adults who manage to 'grow up good.' As your angels change gradually over time, the nature of both their GIMMEEs and their belief systems develop from infantile to mature in several important ways, PROVIDING your children are disciplined wisely. I call these the CHILDHOOD-ADULT MOTIVATIONAL CONTINUUM and the CHILDHOOD-ADULT BELIEF MATURATION CONTINUUM. They are important enough to be charted for you. Read them 100 times. Paste them on your refrigerator next to your angel's snapshots because that is how you start training your muscle-memory toward competent parenting.

CHILDHOOD-ADULT "BELIEF" MATURATION CONTINUUM	
CHILDHOOD BELIEFS	**MATURE BELIEFS**
Beliefs are absolutistic, 100% right vs wrong, black vs white.	Beliefs are flexible; altering with the situation. Gradations exist, with many grays.
I am ALL. I am precious.	I am important, but others exist. Everyone is precious.
Any discomfort is total pain, unbearable. I cannot bear disappointment. I get upset and I can't help it.	Discomfort has many gradations. I can tolerate pain and discomfort while I problem solve with reason intact.
I am a victim. Happiness is an external situation visited upon me.	I am not helpless. I am capable and responsible for what I do and how I think. Happiness is an internal event, mostly under my control.

All WANTS are MUSTS; therefore they may be demanded.	WANTS are not MUSTS. Musts and shoulds are NEEDS, different from WANTS. I like to have my wants, but I do not have to have them. Wants can be requested but not demanded.
I NEED others. I control you.	I don't NEED others. Others are a pleasure to enjoy and treasure, not to use, abuse or control.

CHILDHOOD-ADULT MOTIVATIONAL CONTINUUM	
CHILDHOOD MOTIVATIONAL SYSTEM: MAKE-MY-MOMENT	**MATURE MOTIVATIONAL SYSTEM**
Pleasures are concrete: GIMMEE what I want – food, drink, comfort.	Pleasures are mostly abstract, intrinsic–doing, succeeding, enjoying, sharing, learning.
Pleasures are externally derived... child is totally dependent on the adult for his pleasures, thus a demand characteristic to the GIMMEE pursuit.	Pleasures are mostly self-administered. Adults want to meet their own standards, to feel pride and self-satisfaction. Seeking GIMMEEs from others is enjoyable, but remains a request, not a demand.

Pleasures need to be immediate... MAKE-MY-MOMENTS... NOW! Any delay or interference triggers instant anger. Low frustration tolerance (LFT).	Most pleasures can be delayed for an extensive time, without loss of motivation. Delay of gratification without anger is a valid measure of emotional maturity.
Pleasures are absolutistic in their intensity. 100% happy or 100% miserable. Young child will move from totally peaceful to a screaming bundle of misery in less than a minute.	Pleasures are modulated, show graduations in intensity with a large range of tolerance for discomfort.
Pleasures are non-contingent and non-reciprocal. Adults do not require the child to earn every pleasure nor expect him to pay back tit-for-tat.	Adulthood imposes strict rules of contingency: no one is entitled to something for nothing. Pleasures are to be earned, mostly. Reciprocity is expected. (Be prepared to give back equally if you seek pleasures from others.)

By mid-century the view of Alex, Ashley or Andy as miniature adults was replaced by the psychoexperts with what, to me, seems to have been another dingbat theory of child development. The experts suggested that children are born *TABULA RASA*, fancy Latin words for "blank slate" meaning born free of any temperamental contaminants. Picture this: brand new Alex, pure as snow, available and ready for programming. The psychoexperts boldly declared that, given your angel for the first five years of his life, they could guarantee he would choose to be whatever you desired... sort of like putting in a catalogue order. How about, "Please train me one physician and one engineer" or maybe "one history professor and one astronaut"? Think about that for a minute. Naturally, if we buy that theory, it follows logically that parents would be the culprits if Alex ends up like cantankerous old Uncle Henry and Ashley's parents would be vulnerable for heaps of guilt if their angel ended up anything short of perfection. What an Excedrine headache would be visited upon parents whose stubborn little angel refused to go along with some grand design!

Lucky for us all, the pure *TABULA RASA* theory turned out to be psychobaloney... well, maybe not all baloney, but certainly psychograndiosity. And I guess anybody buying into that kind of grandiosity hasn't yet reckoned with Mother Nature and her tricks. Why, pshaw, any parent with several children could see that their kids had different temperaments and made different responses right from the start. Take my five angels, for example. I remember one time when they were young, all pretty close in age, somebody left a big puddle of dirty snow on the living room rug, and Mother Detective was foolishly searching for a culprit. Each child, when confronted, responded in a unique, characteristic style, no matter who the guilty one. Five kids, five styles. One child would typically respond, "Oh, my gosh, I must have done that... I deserve to have my feet cut off." Another would have said, "Well, not me. I never would do anything like that. See? My boots are dry!" (They were sopping wet.) A third would respond, "What puddle? I don't even see any puddle, Mom." From the fourth, "Well, maybe it WAS me, but it's not my fault, it's yours. You shouldn't have let me come into the house with my boots, Mom." And the last child, "Oh, Mom, what's the big fuss, anyway. So it's a puddle. It's only a little puddle, Mom, and you can clean it up easily." Lucky for me, I ran out of angels after five, but you get the idea. So much for *TABULA RASA* as far as I'm concerned.

BIG DEALS-LITTLE DEALS

I have my own theory... I call it the BIG DEAL-LITTLE DEAL theory. I am convinced kids are just born different. Some come out fighting, full of pizzazz, while others are far less intense, are placid and accommodating. Some have nervous systems that just make big deals out of little deals... you know, the mountain vs the mole hill concept. BIG DEALers grow up catastrophizing about mosquito bites. In fact, they don't even require a real mosquito... they can get upset merely about the IDEA of a mosquito. B. F. Skinner once commented that because people are so much more intelligent than animals they can be one-trial learners. He meant that only one experience, followed by a strong consequence, is enough to cause a learned response. I think he was right, but I believe BIG DEALers didn't even need one real experience... I call them no-trial learners. They learn just by vicarious imagination, while more placid, LITTLE-DEALERS nonchalantly shrug their way through several uncomfortable experiences. That's like the difference between two of my sons, Jack and Jess. One day Jess, placid and accommodating, was bitten by a dog. The very next day, all bandaged, he was back petting dogs again. Jack, more sensitive and contemplative, immediately became dog phobic. See what I mean? Direct experiences do not account totally for individual differences.

HOW DID HE GET THAT WAY?

OKAY! If we toss out the blank slate theory then how can we account for how your angel turns out? What we really mean is, how did Alex, Ashley or Andy get that way and who's to blame? It seems the tendency to blame and shame is the popular way to go these days. Well, never mind the experts. I know the REAL answer, because my mother told me so, in her own, unique way. And it makes sense.

One day, in my own pre-adolescent years, my mother told me that I had a music and art talent. She said I got it from my ancestors and that I was, in fact, a direct descendant of 'Lorenzo the Magnificent,' of Medici fame. Now that didn't mean much to me at my young age, but it tickled my sense of grandiosity and it sure sounded good. Lorenzo the Magnificent! Aawright! But then barely a week later, my mother said to me, "I'll tell you how you got your talent. I made it happen. I named you NORMA after a beautiful Italian opera, and I played classical music next to my tummy and visited many art museums before you were born, and look what happened! You got a talent." "But Mom," I foolishly confronted her, "I thought you said I inherited that from 'Lorenzo the Magnificent.' Now you tell me it is from my earliest environment. I don't understand... and besides, I'm not sure I got anything worth much, because I have only a very modest talent."

And then it was time for my mother to straighten my fuzzy thinking. How foolish of me to confront her. "No," she said, "your problem is not that you did not get a large talent, it is that you have been too lazy and stubborn to develop it"... she paused, then concluded her scientific declaration, "and, unfortunately, you inherited those traits directly from your father."

So there we have it. A perfectly good working hypothesis. Both genes and experiences seem to combine to give each angel his uniqueness. Alex, Ashley and Andy will be some special combination of genes, predisposition, chemistry and experiences. Early experiences weigh heavily, but later ones count too. The BAD NEWS here is that black sheep Uncle Henry might have part of that last laugh! Ashley or Andy might look like him, sound like him, gesture like him or goof like him. The GOOD NEWS is that neither angel will be exactly like Uncle Henry because what parents do certainly does matter. You are not helpless, your angel is not totally predestined and you do not need to suffer misbehavior in him.

So here is my suggested rule. It works great for me and guarantees a NO-GUILT clause. Try it: Blame all your angel's troubles on genes ... not your own of course, your mate's!... and credit all the good he does on your training skills. That way, you never have to feel guilty, but you will feel free to remind yourself that HOW I PARENT COUNTS!

Hopefully, now you have a good mind set to allow you to absorb a quick review and be ready for Chapter B: BABIES KNOW THEIR BUSINESS!

REVIEW: Your angel is precious because he is human.

He is an illogical goof ball and an insatiable GIMMEE machine, his magical G.I. system relentlessly in pursuit of the positive Triple M... MAKE-MY-MOMENT and the negative double D... DIMINISH-MY-DISCOMFORT. At first, he is witless and totally dependent upon you, not only for his real needs, but for all his pleasures. He will take a long time to mature in terms of abstract reasoning and in developing patience and a sense of otherness. At first he is cunning-adorable, but quickly to become cunning-crafty, as well. Get ready: Read Chapter B.

NORMA'S NUGGET:

BABIES ARE NOT MINIATURE ADULTS AND THEY ARE NOT MERELY BLANK SLATES, BUT HOW YOU PARENT COUNTS . . . A LOT.

Chapter B

BABIES KNOW THEIR BUSINESS...

Beginning With the Basics

... A two year old child in an adult body would be more dangerous than a gorilla.
... R. Davis

Baby Andy could not talk yet but he had a basic concept of "NO!" from Mom and Dad. He toddled around and grabbed things and made a bunch of messes, so he must have been around 15 months old. That particular day he was into flushing toilets, his LEMMEEs in high gear. After Andy had pulled the handle about 10 times, Dad had enough. He said "No, Andy, no more," and blocked his baby's pursuit. Well, surprisingly, Andy did not wail in fury. Instead, he gave his Daddy a big smile, pointed up at the ceiling light and grunted. Naturally, Daddy looked up. Quick as a flash, the toilet flushed and Andy laughed, the contest over. His expression said, "I gotcha! My LEMMEEs made me do it." As I recall, a most chagrined Dad came out of the bathroom. "I can't believe what just happened! I have been hornswoggled by a one year old," said he. Said I, "believe it... babies know their business." **Remember the NUGGET:**

BABIES CATCH ON MUCH FASTER THAN YOU CATCH ON THAT THEY HAVE CAUGHT ON!

Chapter B

ANOTHER WAY OF PUTTING IT IS: NEVER UNDERESTIMATE HOW QUICKLY BABIES ADD CUNNING-SMART TO CUNNING-ADORABLE.

About cunning-smart. Did you know that children have 'organized cunning-smart' into a multiple-tiered assault? To my knowledge, no existing book on child development includes what I call the CHILD'S HIERARCHY OF MANIPULATION. Yet no parent I have served ever failed to recognize his child somewhere in this hierarchy. And no child is immune because as long as he is breathing he is actively chasing the TRIPLE M, his tools honed to overcome all resistance. That is the nature of a child's work.

Over many years of observing children and their families I have discerned four major attack styles commonly used by children and they fall into somewhat of a hierarchy. Movement up this ladder appears to depend upon two important factors... your angel's success history of manipulation and his cognitive sophistication.

Cognitively advanced children try more maneuvers a little faster, but sooner or later every child pulls out all the stoppers. I have named these levels to help you recognize and remember them:

Level #1 ... **The EARTHQUAKE**
Level #2 ... **The GUIDED MISSILES**
Level #3 ... **The MOSQUITO BITES**
Level #4 ... **The BIG COLLAPSE**

Level #1: THE EARTHQUAKE

All babies start with the EARTHQUAKE which is the simplest, most primitive GIMMEE demand. Your angel will cry lustily until you give in. Now here's the important point: if this strategy works for your little one he will continue to use it, no matter his age. He does not grow out of a maneuver merely by the passage of time. Just think of all the adults you know who continue to throw some form of temper tantrum when they do not get their way. Some experts have theorized that children who tantrum are signaling a "need" for more attention and therefore must have been deprived of adequate nurturing. While this may be true with neglected and abused children, tantruming should not automatically presume deprivation. Quite the contrary! Adults who throw temper tantrums usually have had an extensive success history in bullying first their parents and later others into compliance, so they continue with the same maneuver... for as long as it works. This is how it develops. Most loving but somewhat anxious parents, especially with their first child, respond instantly to their infant's GIMMEE demands, so baby becomes trained in a very short time to expect a rapid payoff. During the infant months, responding quickly to your angel is totally appropriate, but he develops a strong bent toward wailing instantly for his wants. Whatever works for him becomes the rule and that strategy becomes a habit. By the time your angel toddles he is way ahead in the contest between his GIMMEE demands and your resistance. He will have already experimented with how long or how loud he needs to wail and whether he needs to bring out a fuller arsenal, such as kicking, pounding, throwing and hitting. He might even go for the ultimate weapon, to hold his breath and turn blue. Not all babies will go that far... remember children have different temperaments, one basically more placid than another's. Eventually most parents realize that they had better stop indulging temper tantrums, but they are not confident about when or how to do it. My general rule of thumb for parents is to gutsy up by six months, to start interrupting their angel's total domination. "Beware," I warn, "if you are one of those too tender wimps who cannot stand to see your child thwarted or fear that even mild frustration will signal psychological damage. If so, and you have a strong-willed baby, you are a natural set-up to enter the GORILLA-MAKING business!"

By toddlerhood, it goes like this. Alex demands his GIMMEE or LEMMEE. You refuse him, he cries, you hold out. He cries harder and longer and you try to placate him or distract him while holding firm, to no avail, of course. He pulls out all the stoppers and throws a full tantrum, thrashing violently, especially if you are out in public and somewhat more vulnerable. He might even have to go to that last resort... to stop breathing or choke for a bit. And THEN you give in! Baby smartens up quick. "AHA. Now I get it. I just need to scream louder and longer, cause an enormous fuss, maybe hold my breath a bit, and that will do it!" Voila... the beginnings of a baby gorilla.

Level #2: GUIDED MISSILES

This level has been called THE GUIDED MISSILES because the tantrums are specifically focused upon whomever refuses your angel's GIMMEE-LEMMEE demand. This is slightly more sophisticated than is an EARTHQUAKE eruption in which the anger was explosive but non-directive. In a GUIDED MISSILE Alex screams, "I hate you! You are a mean Mommy ... you are not a fair

Daddy ... I don't love you anymore ... you'll be sorry." You get the picture. If that approach does not bring Mom or Dad to heel, the MISSILE is more finely honed to aim straight at a parent's guilt spot. Now Ashley no longer screams she doesn't love you, but rather that you do not love her. Says she, "you are not a good Mommy... you don't love me anymore... if Daddy loved me he would play with me... Nobody will help me. Nobody loves me!" Be careful now to hear the manipulation. Many a parent may not take seriously a child's angry, "I hate you!" but will feel upset to hear the converse, "You don't love me, Mommy." Adoptive parents and step-parents are particularly vulnerable to this approach. You might be surprised to know how many parents actually feel hurt or unappreciated when their children send GUIDED MISSILES merely because they do not recognize the dedication of a cunning child in strong pursuit of his Triple M. If the shoe fits... if you are vulnerable to an attack of the guilts, what to do? Well, first of all, lighten up and laugh. Remind yourself, "Aha! This is a GUIDED MISSILE." Then imagine yourself reaching for a spray can of Teflon and coat your hide fully. Next, put on a friendly face and go deaf. Do not collapse and indulge the GIMMEE demand. Just as important, do not take that moment to review with your angel all the ways you have been a loving parent. Be not a counselor nor a philosopher. If that is too difficult for you, offer a friendly acknowledgment of his feelings such as, "It is really hard to grow up and learn that you can't always have what you want." And then be quiet. I must warn you... engaging in a dialogue sets the stage for your angel to try the next level.

Level # 3: THE MOSQUITO BITES

Alex and Ashley move to this level after they become fairly verbal and beyond toddlerhood. The attack tones down from angry confrontation to a lower level incessant irritation, which you can remember as the MOSQUITO BITE. Your angels buzz around you. They come at you with childish logic and they NEVER LET UP. They plead, beg, cajole or bargain. You might think of them as training to be lawyers or negotiators. They appeal to your sense of fairness, they assault your logic, they offer propositions: "How come I have to go to bed at 8:30 tonight? Last night you let me stay up later and nothing happened ... I want a $2 raise in my allowance and you don't want to give me any, so how about if we split the difference and I get a $1 raise? ... Jenny gets more money than I do and she doesn't even have to do any work in her house, so why isn't it fair for me to get more? ... How come if I'm not supposed to eat candy YOU eat candy and besides, last week you let me eat some cookies... so what's the difference? ... OK, you aren't going to buy me the new sweater today, but when will you? Tomorrow? Wednesday? How about Saturday? You just don't understand, Mom... I just HAVE TO have that sweater ... everybody else has one and I'll be a weirdo. Is that what you want for me?"... As I said, you begin to feel like a mosquito is nipping you constantly, wearing you down. Now parents who pride themselves on being democratic, fair and open to communication are victimized. Particularly vulnerable are single parents who have allowed their children to relate to them as equal adults. Become aware. Listen for these phrases, which will alert you that a mosquito is buzzing: "Why... ? How come... ? It's not fair... You just don't understand... "

If you can't bring yourself to "slap" at the mosquito

with a firm emphatic "NO!" then try an emphatic "STOP! You are giving me tired ears." I urge you to focus upon your own right to be free from harassment as soon as you recognize that a mosquito is buzzing. I used to tell my kids that no one was allowed to tire my ears for free. My ears could only be rented, for a price. That sounds reasonable, wouldn't you agree? I guess I don't need to add that a mosquito negotiator had better not succeed using this manipulation, lest you never have another moment of golden silence in your lifetime.

Level #4: THE BIG COLLAPSE

This means your child has arrived at the ultimate sophisticated manipulation. Only the strongest of parents do not fall prey to this maneuver unless they have been forewarned. Alex, Ashley and Andy have learned how to really push your button... they need only to stage the BIG COLLAPSE. Alex will droop, hang his head, woefully sad. He says something like, "I'm just no good. No wonder nobody wants me around ... nobody loves me because I am totally worthless ... I don't blame you for not wanting to help me (sigh), I don't deserve it. I'm just a loser." Something like that. Truly depressed children need to be taken seriously, of course, but you might notice under what conditions your angel pulls his collapse. If Alex or Ashley energetically pursue their TRIPLE M and collapse only when they are being thwarted, you can make a good educated guess that they are trying to manipulate you into owning the responsibility for making their life easy and comfortable.

When Alex and Ashley have become verbal and sophisticated enough to use a complete arsenal of manipulation, they will pick and choose strategies according to the situation, moving up and down the hierarchy as needed. This is just another way of saying that no matter what their age, BABIES KNOW THEIR BUSINESS!

MEET THE 'AINS'

A famous wit, Mell Lazarus once concluded... "the secret of dealing successfully with a child is not to be its parent." He may be right, but probably now you're stuck with the job. You need some tools to stand a fighting chance in the contest between you and your baby gorilla. "Don't despair," I tell parents, "all is fair in love and war and gorilla-bashing." So let me introduce you to the 'AINS,' my foolproof strategy for establishing you firmly in charge of your angels. The 'AINS' include: EXPLAIN ... TRAIN ... REMAIN ... REFRAIN. I made them rhyme, all the better to help you firm them in your memory and pop them out of your brain instantly as needed. If you will use these four AINs appropriately and consistently your little angel will 'grow up good' and there will be no gorillas living in your home.

EXPLAIN... You probably know the common jokes about the farmer and his donkey, but please be patient. I especially like two of them and the first goes with EXPLAIN.

The farmer had a donkey he was trying to sell. A prospective buyer inquired about whether the animal was stubborn. "I want a donkey that will obey me," he insisted. The farmer smiled. "No problem with this donkey. He is very obedient. I'll show you." He strapped a burden on the donkey and ordered it to walk. The donkey moved not at all. The farmer raised his voice, commanding the donkey once again, but to no avail. The animal remained motionless, seemingly nonchalant. So the farmer picked up a board and cracked it over the donkey's head, after which the animal began to walk at a good pace. "But my word!" exclaimed the horrified buyer, "you said this donkey was obedient!" "And he is," responded the farmer, "but first you have to get his attention."

EXPLAIN means communicating a request or a directive to your child and making sure that your angel has heard the message clearly and understands it. Think about driving your car and coming upon a yellow traffic light. The yellow light has a specific purpose, which is to get your attention, to alert you that a very definite rule is about to go into effect... that in five seconds the light will turn red and then you must stop your car. The yellow light does not train, in itself. It merely signals what is to happen next. If you continue to drive while the light is yellow, no consequence occurs and you are allowed to pursue your automotive LEMMEE without interference. The sole purpose of the yellow light is to alert and this is precisely what I mean by the word EXPLAIN. In communicating with children, unlike donkeys, it makes sense to use language, rather than action, when signaling a YELLOW LIGHT. We all know that a child will be more agreeable if a parent explains not only the rule but why it is necessary. Successful EXPLAINING includes keeping your message clear and specific, not too wordy and monitoring your tone to sound firm but kind. Being firm does not mean stern and doesn't include harsh, threatening commands. No one wants to be ordered around like an animal. That only makes a child feel humiliated and invites him to become stubborn.

Just as firm should not be confused with stern, however, neither does 'kind' equate with 'weak.' A directive will carry no credibility if it is delivered as a timid request that might be allowed to be refused or ignored by your angel. In other words, don't send a RED LIGHT 'STOP' directive in a wimpish tone that invites a GREEN LIGHT 'GO.'

An effective EXPLAIN requires more than the right tone, of course. The message also needs to be precise and concrete. Children do not respond well to ambiguity. When they are young they don't understand it and then when they do, ambiguity generates a wellspring of loopholes for those mosquito-negotiators! Your angel needs to hear exactly what you are requesting. To tell Ashley to "be a good girl" is not useful. She needs to hear specifically, "Ashley, I need you to play by yourself until I have finished washing the dishes." Again, to request Alex to "go clean your room" is not a clear YELLOW LIGHT. Define what you mean by a clean room. Do you mean make the bed? Put dirty clothes in the hamper? Does it include putting toys on a shelf, or in a box? If Alex is quite young, he might need a list on his wall with stick pictures to denote each task. Then, always be sure that your angel has heard you and understood you. The best guarantee is to have him repeat and explain the directive back to you. Last and most importantly... once you are sure your angel understands your directive, NEVER KEEP REPEATING IT. Do not substitute a repeating YELLOW LIGHT for a RED LIGHT. A real YELLOW LIGHT moves to RED automatically. A RED LIGHT means a training program is now in effect. Be not a wimp! Let your YELLOW LIGHT turn RED.

TRAIN... Here's that second farmer-donkey story. It goes with TRAIN. Two farmers were trudging to market with their donkeys. One donkey stumbled and the farmer muttered, "that's once." After awhile, the donkey stumbled again and the farmer announced, "that's twice." They continued to market. A short ways along, the unfortunate donkey stumbled a third time, whereupon the farmer took out a gun and shot the animal. "Good grief!" exclaimed the other man. "What in the world did you do that for?" The first farmer looked him straight in the eye, "that's once."

TRAIN means the YELLOW LIGHT has turned RED and now a training program with consequences automatically goes into effect. No IF'S or BUT'S! TRAIN is very different from EXPLAIN because TRAIN means action, not words. In EXPLAIN you are careful to say what you mean, but now in TRAIN you must prove to your child that you mean what you say... once you announce a declaration you must follow through, even if that requires real effort. Let me demonstrate with a true, personal example:

I remember taking grandson Andy, age 3, to the Mall. As we entered, we could see the great expanse of open corridors. Instinctively, I gave Andy a YELLOW LIGHT. "Please stay next to me. Do not run away." Andy obeyed for about 10 seconds, until the lure of his LEMMEE juices took over and he bolted. Since I had already given him a YELLOW LIGHT directive, a RED LIGHT action needed to follow. So I did what any modern Grandma in sneakers would do... I took off after him, and afraid that he could scoot faster than I, tackled him right in the middle of the Mall. "Grandma," spluttered Andy, "why did you do that?" I picked up both of us with as much dignity as I could muster and in a CALM voice replied, "because you forgot what I told you. You must not run away from me in this big place." I had said what I meant, so I had to mean what I said. And this time I made sure that he could tell me the 'rule' before we continued.

Hopefully you will not have to invoke such heroics very often, but the hard lesson here is that you may not relish the inconvenience required to follow through immediately with an action. Remember, both children and adults have G.I. juices constantly in operation and often you just DONWANNA confront your angel with an action. Maybe you're a confirmed wimp. Maybe you are tired and it's too much trouble to enact the RED LIGHT consequence. Or maybe you think your angel didn't understand and that you need only to EXPLAIN once again. You might feel guilty or cruel if you take a firm action, believing that 'good parents' should remain patient and discuss issues with a child. Hey... discussing issues is an excellent parenting principle, but NOT in the middle of a YELLOW LIGHT-RED LIGHT sequence. Timing is so important! Remember Andy in the Mall. I EXPLAINED a second time, but only AFTER I had followed through with an action.

Often parents come to me when one sibling bullies another. When I inquire, for example, "What do you do immediately after Bobby hits his little brother?," a parent typically responds, "I always EXPLAIN to him why he must not do that, that it hurts his brother and that it is not fair. But telling him never seems to work!" Of course not. That poor mother did not understand the difference between a YELLOW LIGHT and RED LIGHT, so she had no training program in effect. Well, actually she did... a totally ineffective one. Her sequence was to follow each misbehavior with an automatic reset YELLOW LIGHT. She thought she was being a good mother, patiently explaining again and again to her child, assuming that when he truly understood, he would alter his behavior. Instead, she was accidentally allowing a baby gorilla to develop in the family. We learn by consequences. EXPLAINING is not a good consequence. Very gradually, we all learn to choose how we will behave according to the consequences we anticipate. Unfortunately, children are terrible at anticipating consequences when they are young. They just pursue their GIMMEEs and LEMMEEs and IDONWANNAs aware only of that Triple-M: MAKE-MY-MOMENT. When Bobby hit his younger brother, he needed to experience a consequence such as sitting in his room, removed from pleasures, and the action needed to be immediate. Only later should any further discussion take place and ONLY THEN if you are convinced that Bobby truly did not 'understand.'

If Bobby is a continual bully, even after logical and consistent consequences are carried out, then you have a different situation to be explored; to discover if Bobby is deliberately pursuing a PERVERSE PLEASURE, enjoying the hurt he inflicts. If so, that indicates he is not 'growin' up good' and you need to consult some professional help. Some parents spoil their TRAIN with foolish threats such as, "if you do that again, I'll kill you!," or "if you fail to do your homework one more time, no TV for a year." Foolish because you are unlikely to carry out such consequences. You don't really mean what you say... at least I hope not!

The more a parent has mastery of both the EXPLAIN program and the TRAINing consequences, the faster the learning. Parents have much better control of a young child's environment than an older child's, for sure, as any parent of a teenager will attest. That is why almost every child expert advises parents to train early. Gorilla prevention is much easier than gorilla bashing. That is, it is much easier, providing a child can understand a request and that the request is appropriate for his ability to respond. It would be foolish and unfair to ask your angel for behavior beyond reason for his age and understanding, but it almost never too soon to insist kindly but firmly that even a young toddler obey your YELLOW-turn-RED LIGHT.

UNDERSTANDING CONSEQUENCES

Before we leave TRAIN, a word to clear up some confusion about the concept of consequences. Today some popular child-rearing books tell parents not to use punishment, but consequences instead. Now that is a technically incorrect and confusing message, because punishment is one form of consequence. POSITIVE REWARD is another. Both reward and punishment are consequences, pure and simple, and both procedures prove to be effective in training. If your child engages in a behavior and a consequence follows immediately, either positive or negative, learning takes place. The more powerful, more immediate, more concrete and more consistent the consequence, the faster and more firmly the training occurs. Many child experts suggest that parents use only positive consequences in their training; a phrase commonly offered is 'catch your child being good.' In this approach, parents are urged to limit themselves to positive rewards such as praise, smiles, hugs, and smiley faces and to simply ignore misbehavior which should gradually extinguish if never rewarded. In the world of everyday living, however, ignoring is not always practical, and in reality, research has proved that a combining of both positive and negative consequences is more effective. Appropriate feedback following both acceptable behavior and misbehavior makes salient to a child the cause-and-effect relationship between his behavior and its consequences. There is no question that punishment trains effectively. To the contrary, it can be too effective and thus needs to be employed with caution, so there are some caveats to be considered. Mother Nature specializes in punishment consequences. If a child touches a hot stove and he feels pain, he very quickly experiences learning. He does not like the feedback and he may become afraid of the stove, but he does not 'hate' the stove nor personalizes the pain as an attack on his worth or lovability. Unfortunately, there is an enormous difference between Mother Nature and people as trainers.

That is why many experts recommend avoiding punishment as a training device and that is why you need to fully understand the next two AINS: REMAIN and REFRAIN.

REMAIN and REFRAIN... Have you ever seen a YELLOW LIGHT get upset? How about a RED LIGHT? Of course not. The YELLOW LIGHT is not interested in your unique problems. It cares not one whit whether you have had a trying day with your boss, or are late for dinner. It cares not one whit whether you are happy, depressed or dog-tired. It REMAINS unimpassioned, no matter if you swear, scream, cry, beg or cajole... the YELLOW LIGHT simply turns RED, and the RED LIGHT begins its consequence program. Traffic lights do not get upset and do not match or join you in your emotional upheaval. They remain calm and unimpressed. And that is the magic phrase to remember throughout both EXPLAIN and TRAIN: REMAIN CALM AND UNIMPRESSED. Be not upset when your child is behaving... of all things... just like a child... relentlessly pursuing his GIs. Remember, that is his nature! Your goal is to TRAIN your angel away from gorillahood and therefore you will need to interrupt those G.I. juices quite often. Count on it and count on his becoming upset when you block him. If you join him in his upsettedness, however, you only derail the TRAIN program, because your angel will immediately stop focusing on his misbehavior and attend to your emotionality. Now that cunning-smart little gorilla shifts to the offensive position, the spotlight off him and on you. Says he, "I don't care what I did! You shouldn't yell at me. You hurt my feelings!" No longer is it relevant to Bobby that he had hit his brother. Now, in his head, his own misbehavior has been dismissed.

I have long pondered what it requires for parents to REMAIN calm and unimpressed when their child misbehaves and to REFRAIN from attack. This is what I have concluded. Parents can REMAIN calm and unimpressed if they hold a firm belief that their child will turn out OK eventually and they can hope for this if they recognize a misbehavior for exactly what it is... a child with a huge G.I. system in operation but without enough common sense to balance it. I remember asking one very upset parent what ideas she held in her head to cause such a strong reaction when her son Jeffrey failed to complete his homework. Our survey of her head-talk went something like this... "If he doesn't do his homework, that means he will hang around with the wrong kids and get into trouble, and then end up on drugs and go to jail, and ruin his life." No wonder that Mother found it impossible to remain unimpressed! She made an unfounded leap from a typical child misbehavior to a dire prediction of disaster. A second way for parents to REMAIN calm is for them to discipline themselves to automatically let a YELLOW LIGHT turn RED after only ONE EXPLAIN, without repeats. Almost all parents I know who get upset have a bad habit of resetting a YELLOW LIGHT not just once, but over and over, until they become so exasperated that they lose their cool. Only then do they turn on a RED LIGHT, but of course they are already too upset to talk in a firm but kind way. What they are doing is training their angel to listen not to a reasonably spoken clear YELLOW LIGHT, but to watch and listen for a different YELLOW LIGHT, namely their parent's upsettedness gauge. And who knows, that gauge might vary from day to day, depending upon Mother or Dad's own G.I. juices.

Once, many years ago, I was talking to my neighbor, a sweet and loving wimp, at the curb. Her five-year-old Jenny kept running into the street while we chatted. In a pleading voice Mother said, "Please don't do that, Jenny." Jenny ignored her and went into the street, while Mother continued chatting. After a minute, Mother said again, "Stop, Jenny. Please don't go into the street." But she took no action and the YELLOW LIGHT had again been reset. I counted seven resets. Finally Mother became frustrated and shouted, "I said, don't go into that street and if you set one toe off this curb I will spank you!" Then Jenny behaved. The child responded to what she now perceived as a YELLOW LIGHT turned RED. But Mother was upset, embarrassed and angry. Next, Jenny cried and Mother immediately became apologetic and consoling.

What a mess! Jenny had not learned to obey a mother who could remain both calm and firm at the same time. The real training program in effect was: do whatever you want, no matter what I say, until I get mad. Then get upset and put the focus back on me.

Mother's apology introduces REFRAIN, which goes hand-in-hand with REMAIN. While REMAIN focuses upon a parent's emotional response, REFRAIN mediates your verbal behavior. Not only do traffic lights remain calm, they REFRAIN from offering verbal feedback to the errant driver. A yellow light does not attempt to RE-EXPLAIN why a rule is important and certainly does not assume it can turn red only if the driver agrees the rule is fair! Neither does it apologize nor seek forgiveness for 'causing' the driver to feel upset. In tandem, after a driver misbehaves, the red light does not apologize for carrying out a consequence. Even more importantly, the red light does not condemn, attack or try to shame the driver into better behavior. No character assassination... a distinction so often lost by parents who punish in anger.

While Mother Nature can teach effectively by a strong and immediate punishment consequence, parents need to understand that people trainers may not get the same expected outcome. Any form of punishment that attacks the child may stop a misbehavior, but almost always creates a different problem. Children trained by hitting, shaming, ridiculing, nagging, criticizing or condemning seldom 'grow up good.' Angry parents frighten children. If under constant attack, they may obey, but either they will not grow to think clearly without intrusion of fear or they may rebel against authority figures. Such children develop a whole new set of GIMMEEs and IDONWANNAs, namely the pursuit of perverse pleasures presented in

Chapter A such as getting even, bullying others, engaging in 'I GOTCHA' power struggles or even worse, downright cruelty. They stop pursuing positive pleasures in a healthy way and thus do not grow into loving, caring people.

Even children who are not physically punished but subjected to verbal assaults cannot escape the side-effects, which is low self-esteem, because they cannot distinguish between criticism of their behavior and criticism of their total being. Most child guidance experts suggest that you take particular care to tell your misbehaving angel, "I dislike your behavior but not you." But do you know what? I think you might as well be whistling in the wind! Even under the most gentle of approaches, children cannot grasp that subtle distinction between "I don't like you" and "I don't like your behavior." And they most certainly confuse that difference if you violate REFRAIN and scold or nag angrily. Remember an important point from Chapter A? Children think concretely, drawing conclusions in absolutistic, all-or-nothing terms. Therefore my suggestion is that you REFRAIN even from saying, "Your behavior is bad" to a child. After he has hit his little brothers, say to Bobby, instead, "Stop! You may not do that. You need to go to your room right now and stay there until I come and get you. No hitting younger children." Later, you can tell your child, "I know it is hard to remember the rule but I love you and it is my job to help you 'grow up good'."

Well, there you have it. I promised you simple and simple it is: For effective gorilla prevention, you need only imitate a traffic light! Can that be any simpler?

Here is a summary of the 'AINS' RULES. If you do not get anything else out of this book, get this page! Cut it out and hang it on your refrigerator. Review it every day for a few minutes until you can respond as automatically as a traffic light, with EXPLAIN ... TRAIN ... REMAIN and REFRAIN.

EXPLAIN ... TRAIN ... REMAIN ... REFRAIN

EXPLAIN . . .

Give a clear and simple directive in a kind but firm voice. Make sure the child has understood and can repeat what you are requesting. This is the YELLOW LIGHT. Do not keep repeating your request. Let the YELLOW LIGHT turn RED.

TRAIN . . .

Stop talking and take an action. This is crucial. You must follow through with a consequence, immediately after the child has failed to obey a RED LIGHT. Try to do it every time, consistently, while you are training. Stay pleasant but hold the child accountable for his misbehavior in some way. Do not substitute "talking to him about his misdeed" for an action consequence. In fact, do no talk to him about the misbehavior until much later, if at all. Always the consequence before the 'talk-through.'

REMAIN . . .

REMAIN deals with your emotionality. REMAIN CALM and UNIMPRESSED. If you become emotional, the spotlight moves away from the child, where it belongs and lands on you. Unimpressed does not mean uncaring or indifferent. It means staying pleasant but resolute ... understanding, but firm and calm.

REFRAIN . . .

REFRAIN works in tandem with REMAIN but deals with your verbal responses to your child's misbehavior. REFRAIN from attacking your child. Please discipline yourself and resist a strong urge to lecture, cajole, criticize, ridicule or cast dire predictions about future catastrophes. Remember to let the RED LIGHT program do the training.

Oh, I think I forgot to mention one last AIN... COMPLAIN! And this is exactly what you will do for the rest of your life if you allow your child to 'grow up gorilla.'

NORMA'S NUGGET:

SAY ONLY WHAT YOU MEAN, THEN MEAN WHAT YOU SAY. DO IT IN A FIRM BUT KIND STYLE. REMEMBER KIND DOES NOT MEAN WIMP, NOR DOES FIRM MEAN STERN.

Chapter 

COMMON-SENSE CONSIDERATIONS

... There may be some doubt as to who are
the best people to have charge of children,
but there can be no doubt that parents are the worst.
. . . G. B. Shaw

Have you ever heard of a CSQ? Probably not, because I invented it one day while trying to teach a resistant parent about rules and flexibility. CSQ stands for COMMON-SENSE QUOTIENT. As I mentioned in the Introduction, I am convinced that the phrase 'COMMON-SENSE' really means a special kind of practical wisdom which develops only from plenty of experience and a flexible viewpoint. The term is a misnomer, of course, in that common-sense proves to be a scarce commodity. After all, how many truly sensible people do you know?

Common-sense is not to be confused with intelligence. I know Ph.D.s who are scholarly whizzes but don't know when to come in from the rain, and have no idea how they are perceived by other people. I am still struggling with how to rename COMMON-SENSE. I thought about SENIOR SENSE, where you kind of mellow your way into wisdom through an abundance of living. But that doesn't quite do it. After all, everyone knows the expression 'there's no fool like an old fool.' Maybe old fools are people who keep practicing foolishness over and again, locked into such a rigid way of thinking that they can't adjust to changing conditions. For sure, I think common-sense must include flexibility in wisdom. And flexibility reminds me of a story... not one of my favorite old jokes this time, but a true report.

> *An official for a high school wrestling match was weighing-in the student wrestlers on the locker room scale. The athletes had been instructed, as always, to follow the rule to wear only a jock-strap for the weigh-in. This year, however, a novel situation developed. A few excellent girl athletes had earned berths on the wrestling team, for the first time in the school's history. When the girls arrived for a separate weigh-in, they had substituted a light bra and panties for the traditional jock strap. But alas, the official disqualified them. Why? Because they had failed to follow the rules of dress!*

See what I mean? Maybe we can't define common-sense precisely, but we sure know when it is missing!

For me, common-sense meant Grandma. When I was a child and my Grandma found me upset, she always asked the same question, "Did you kill anyone?" When I would answer, "No, but... " she would interrupt with an exaggerated sigh of relief and say, "Well now, that's good! We can fix anything else." How I wish that all adults raising children could wise-up with advancing age as automatically as we wrinkle! But, as the wrestling official demonstrated, some people seem to get it, and some just don't.

Young children do not have ANY common-sense and

that is a given. We know that your angels start at zero on the common-sense scale. They drink poison, touch light sockets, and wander into swimming pools. They tell Grandma she has ugly wrinkles in her face and repeat all the family secrets in school at SHOW 'N TELL. They spend an entire week's allowance on candy and leave their brand new bicycle out in the rain. Such is the essence of childhood. Kids can't think past the end of their noses... and they have very short noses. They don't grasp the BIG picture, always missing some important elements. So one main task in helping your angels 'grow up good' is finding how they can gain wisdom with flexibility. It stands to reason that if you want to develop common-sense in your Alex, Ashley or Andy you need to meet two conditions: first, check out your own common-sense in dealing with your child... are you a common-sense parent? A ding-bat parent almost guarantees ding-bat kids; second, you need to allow your child to practice making decisions independently, again and again, even when he makes mistakes, because that allows him to learn from natural consequences. After all, in order to learn from experiences, a child must HAVE experiences!

I remember one parent who never let her eight-year-old daughter take even one step freely around her close neighborhood because she was afraid her child might encounter some problem. Yet this mother was bringing her for evaluation because the child had no ability to make decisions and lacked confidence, and mother wondered why.

Even parents generally thought to have common sense can lose that precious commodity. I must confess I have. Adolescents, especially, can make that happen to us quite easily, as I well recall:

...My son Tony was in high school. Sometime during his senior year Tony's LEMMEE-IDONWANNA juices acted as if he had already graduated, when in reality, his carcass had yet to attend one last semester. Well, Tony began to show up late for his first morning class. Now his school had a reasonable expectation that pupils belonged in class on time, and a tardiness policy that required a note of explanation. Failure to bring one dictated that a pupil could not return to school until accompanied by a parent ... Tony had no problem with that rule, in principle, but suddenly he was giving himself permission to arrive late on a fairly regular basis. As you might guess, I was not happy to be forced to school on behalf of Tony's LEMMEE-IDONWANNA juices, particularly since I was a working parent and Tony was a good student, ready to graduate. So... I committed my first common-sense violation. I wrote a note, falsely excusing Tony for his lateness. I let him (and me) off the hook. A few days later Tony told me he had been late again, and would need another note. I hated inventing 'false' excuses, but wrote the note to avoid the pesky consequence. That was my second mistake. A week later the incident repeated and I blew my cool. Feeling more than a little guilty for my collusion, I screamed at him to remember this would be my 'final' note... and that he could expect

no more notes unless he were dead! And so I wrote the false excuse. No other action on my part, you understand, except to scold... and wimp out. In actuality I had just reset the third YELLOW LIGHT. Well, the results could have been anticipated. Before long he was late once again, and came to ask for that required entry note.

This time I remembered EXPLAIN-TRAIN-REMAIN and REFRAIN. I did not scream or carry-on. I merely sighed and acknowledged that I had better acquiesce since I did not want the consequence of accompanying him to school. I wrote, sealed and gave him the note.

That night Tony came home from school, most chagrined. "Mom, how could you do such a thing to me?" "I had to, Tony," I explained, "I finally figured out how to give YOU the consequence and not me." My note had read, "Please excuse Tony's absence yesterday. He couldn't help it, he died." My common-sense and humor had returned... a bit late, perhaps, but not too late. Finally I had taken an action instead of resetting the now famous 'YELLOW-LIGHT.' Whereas all my scolding and threatening had failed to alter Tony's behavior, a simple action, without emotionality or personal attack brought results. Tony never asked me for another note... and he graduated, by the way.

So now the big question. Why did I parent so poorly? I knew better. Where was my common-sense? Sincere parents often ask me to help them understand why they continue to parent foolishly even when they recognize what they are doing. Good question, and it has required years of watching and listening before I could formulate an adequate response. No doubt parents lose their common-sense for many reasons... and some never had much to lose, but I have observed three types of foolishness that consistently cross my professional door. One I call the G.I. CONFLICTS; another, the overdose POISON PILLS; and the last, PSYCHOBABBLE MISEDUCATION. Mull them over, one at a time and think about whether any of the shoes fit you.

GIMMEE-IDONWANNA CONFLICTS

Parents after all, are human. I know I get tired and cranky and discouraged, sometimes. So our own GIMMEEs and IDONWANNAs just plain get in the way of common sense, since good parenting will require persistence and inevitable confrontation. With Tony, we saw how my IDONWANNA overrode common-sense and that I indulged myself until I recognized that my foolishness was hurting him. I had correctly observed that the intended negative consequence was going to be more problematic for me, the parent, than for Tony, the culprit... which by the way, is never a good consequence program. With humor, however, I managed to turn the consequence away from me and onto him, exactly where it belonged. If this shoe fits and you tend to let your own GIs prevent common-sense, remember that taking the 'easy way out' of a confrontation will prove to make life much more difficult for you and your child in the long run. NUGGET: MOMENTARY DIMINUTION OF DISCOMFORT FOR YOU IS NOT WORTH THE PRICE LATER.

Some GIMMEE-LEMMEE conflicts between parent and child, unfortunately, are not just temporary aberrations but can grow from a perverse motivational system. One parent came for help because life with her child had become unbearable. They were locked into a power-struggle, very similar to what had occurred with her own mother twenty years earlier. In fact, that generational battle was not yet over. She could admit that she actually hated her mother and was still angry about her constant bossiness. But when I suggested to this young mother that she interrupt the vicious cycle and let go of bossing her own child, she became visibly upset. "But I never got my turn! When do I get to be the boss? My mother said it would be my turn when I grew up. If I don't boss my child, then I get cheated!" That poor woman was a victim of a G.I. system gone awry. Perverse pleasures provided her motivation and clearly lowered her common-sense quotient.

POISON PILLS

While some parents fall prey to G.I. conflicts, I have observed that most parents are willing to endure discomfort while training their child. In fact, too many of you suffer from just the opposite dilemma, and administer an overdose of parenting under the mistaken notion that if some monitoring of children is good, then more monitoring must be better. Your common-sense disappears if you cannot discriminate between ENOUGH and TOO MUCH. Excessive parenting is like an overdose of pills. Everybody knows that too much of even the best medication can be hurtful. And so it is with parenting. I call these excessive intrusions poison pills in that they cause parents, unintentionally, to poison the process of 'growin' up good.' These poison pills include: over-protection, over-correction, over-indulgence and over-involvement... any of which guarantee over reactive responses.

If you are a parent who overprotects or overcorrects you tend to be excessively anxious, perhaps holding irrational ideas about the nature of your child and about your proper role. Overprotective parents commonly hold the notion that a child is as fragile as glass, quick to shatter under duress... or like a popsicle, vulnerable to melting or collapsing. Overly protective parents do not trust that a child is psychologically robust enough to handle obstacles and disappointments.

The problem of discriminating between 'enough' and 'too much' invades common-sense. No reasonable parent would allow his angel to be crushed by boulder size problems, but overly anxious parents cannot separate boulders from pebbles. You fear that if Alex encounters a negative experience he will suffer a setback in his development, so you tend to walk ahead of him, picking all the pebbles from his path. Holding that view and feeling responsible for Alex's development, you can do no less than keep a nonstop vigil.

Why is it poisonous to prevent negative experiences whenever possible, you might inquire? Is that not what a caring parent should do? Alas, a paradox. Parents want their angel to feel strong and brave and powerful, but an overprotected child turns out just the opposite! He becomes fearful, not only of boulders, not only of pebbles, but soon even of imaginary pebbles, He feels weak and helpless, which is definitely in the opposite direction from 'growin' up good.' He doesn't get enough opportunities to feel brave and to practice problem solving independently, so he gradually displays the very behaviors that worry you... lack of judgment, poor self-esteem and no grit. We might call it a 'parent-fulfilling prophecy,' in that everyone gradually comes to describe this child as vulnerable, overly tender and needing protection.

Some parents are overprotective out of guilt or pity. If this shoe fits you, probably your head-talk runs, "My poor baby, life is so cruel and unfair. I owe him. I must provide him with pleasure and shield him from hurt. This script is quite common in parents who are divorced or have a handicapped child. While understandable, the notion lacks common-sense because if you fail to hold your child accountable for reasonable behavior, soon he will have two problems... the original one plus poor coping skills. Not only will your angel be fearful, but he is likely to become demanding. Of all contributing factors, probably guilt and pity prove to be the greatest gobblers of parental CSQ. You will have a hard time believing this absolutely true anecdote:

> *Marty's parents came in despair. Their eleven-year-old son was not well coordinated and had few, if any friends. So Dad was appointed to fill the deficit, as they explained, "lest Marty's self-esteem diminish." The problem was that Dad was not succeeding. He believed he was responsible, but admitted that he was feeling not*

only angry but also guilty because he was not enjoying this special 'father-son' program. Every night Marty was waiting at the door for Dad to arrive home from work. No matter if Dad was tired or wished to relax a bit, he felt morally responsible to throw a ball with Marty until dinner, even though Marty would criticize his father's efforts. Immediately after dinner, Marty and Dad would play cards or games in the basement so Marty could have those social interactions so important for a pre-adolescent boy. It turned out that Marty often cheated, which Dad chose to ignore, because "poor Marty was feeling so bad about himself," said Dad. Even worse, if Dad tried to confront him or if Marty did not win the game, he would throw the cards on the floor and overturn the game table. Dad decided this would be so upsetting to Marty that he had better let his son win every game. I asked Dad if he had ever considered just letting Marty be upset, and telling him that if he cheated or threw cards Dad would stop playing for that night? To my surprise, Dad said, "Yes... " and then added, "but I only tried that once. It didn't work." I pursued, "How is that? Could you not have just gone upstairs and walked away?" "No," said Dad, "I tried that, but as I climbed the stairs Marty bit my leg. I figured he was really upset, so now I can't leave."

So help me, that was a true incident. As I said, guilt and pity take the prize for eroding common-sense. I see many Martys, years later, still trying to 'grow up good,' but now facing the difficult task of reprogramming themselves. It's never too late, fortunately, just more difficult.

Now, about that poison pill: Overcorrection. Some parents are less concerned about their child experiencing discomfort, but are very anxious about whether he can develop into a moral, responsible person without punitive discipline. They believe the old saw that to 'spare the rod spoils the child.' Expecting a child to lie and cheat, they keep a vigilant monitoring of his private interests ... his plans, his phone calls, his letters, hoping to intercept trouble. Although overcorrecting parents mean well they cross the line between common-sense parenting and meddling. This overanxiety stems from an irrational belief that a childish misbehavior is a sign of impending disaster, a catastrophe in the making. Remember Jeffrey's mother, in the last chapter, so overwrought because he had sneaked away from his homework just one night? That transgression bought him an overkill punishment, not because Mom was cruel, but because she wanted to prevent him from "going to jail." She was caught in the 'pebble-boulder' dilemma, this time in discriminating between a pebble-sized child misbehavior and a boulder-sized character disorder. If this shoe fits you, check out your assumptions. Are you scripting a nightmare in your head and responding to it as a reality? Once again, the paradox; a child with over-controlling parents, similar to overprotective parents, is likely to exhibit the very behaviors you struggle so hard to prevent. Children who have not been trusted, victims of parental intrusion and character assassination often become manipulative liars.

They may not start out that way, but gradually grow into the role as they despair of escaping the ever-relentless parental inquisitions. Life with an overly intrusive parent can become such a hassle that the child learns to 'shade the truth' as a survival technique. Even a child as young as seven or eight will tell me, "I decided I might as well do it, because my Mom and Dad wouldn't believe me anyway."

A third kind of poison pill is overspecialing your angel, either with GIMMEE indulgences or excessive attention. Common-sense dictates that it is not good for a child to be overly indulged in toys or privileges without some contributing effort from the child. "Why not?," some parents protest, especially those who themselves had few luxuries early in life. "Why not, if I can afford it? I like to see them happy." One wealthy parent proudly stated to me that his life's desire was to provide financially so well for his son that the boy would never have to work a day in his life. How unfortunate! That father could not see that his own sense of strength and confidence had derived from meeting personal challenges. Providing a rainbow of free pleasures almost assuredly would prohibit his angel from developing either inner strength or a sense of appreciation.

Excessive indulgences in material pleasures can make it difficult to keep your child motivated by his own efforts. Even more insidious, however, is overspecialing your angel with attention and praise, a surprising revelation to well-intentioned parents who have been trained to believe that giving a child an abundance of time and interest is the 'right' thing to do. It is, but once again, common-sense dictates moderation. Your Alex, Ashley and Andy also need practice in learning how to amuse themselves, how to be comfortable even when alone, without expecting an adult to be in attendance. I see dozens of children who cannot or will not do homework unless a parent remains by their side, and parents unable to hold even a short conversation between themselves without their angel bidding intrusively for attention. Not only does that child demand attention, but insists upon receiving strokes and praise. How does such a child survive when he leaves his parents' adulation to become only one of many kindergarten children who must share a teacher's time and attention? The answer is, not very well! Perplexed parents will complain to me, "I don't know why my child's teacher doesn't seem to like him. He is so adorable at home..I think the problem is the teacher... she just doesn't understand my individual child and what he needs." And then my unwelcome response, "Is it possible that you have accidentally programmed this problem by declaring your child too special and have taught him to expect non-stop personal attention? That is not what he needs, but merely what he wants and has come to expect."

Try on that shoe. If it fits, you have confused your child's WANTs with his NEEDs. What your angel does not need is a personal butler at his beckoning. If this child lives in your house, increase your CSQ and begin immediately to wean him from excessive attention. Be very careful not to conclude that a child's misbehavior signals a 'need' for more attention nor indicates that he is not yet 'ready' for independence. Entitlement is such an important topic that it is more fully examined in Chapter E.

The other poison pill that conflicts with your CSQ might be called over-attachment, and tends to occur when you think of your angel as an extension of you. I still laugh about an old cartoon I once saw. Picture a four-year old boy in his backyard standing stiffly in his snowsuit. He was so excessively bundled that he could not possibly bend over to play in the snow. The caption read, "My mother had a chill."

Often over-attached parents have their own worth on the line and live vicariously through their child's accomplishments. They react to their angel's every production, good or bad, elated about a perfect spelling paper, and upset by a poor one. If a teacher accidentally mis-marks the child's paper, the parent is at the teacher's door to correct the error, sometimes angrily. If Ashley genuinely earns a bad grade, a volcano of consequences erupts; privileges are curtailed, and stringent monitoring invades the homework program. The implicit message delivered to the child is that it is incumbent upon her to bring pride to her parents, not just herself. Somewhere along the way, Ashley begins to feel that she will not be a good person if she fails to follow a plan designed for her.

I remember well a young medical doctor in my office struggling with a major depression. He hated being a doctor and confessed that he never had wanted to go to medical school. When I inquired why he had pursued such a taxing career in which he had held no interest, he explained that his father had saved for many years to earn the tuition, so he felt duty bound to honor his father's dream. Another young man I knew well was playing on my son's football team. One day he dropped a crucial pass, causing his team to lose the game. His father was enraged, declaring that his son had humiliated him. "Whoa!" I tell such a parent. Take a good look at yourself and your CSQ. If you have an image problem, go fix it... don't dump it on your child." It is a hard lesson to grasp that your child is not an extension of you. He may be expected to show respect and appreciation of your devotion but he does not owe you accolades, as if they can be transferred from his own life choices onto your self-worth. Take care. Children who come to believe that they must achieve in order to please parents do not tend to 'grow up good.' Instead, they spend a lifetime anguishing in the pursuit of inner peace.

PSYCHOBABBLE MISEDUCATION

Psychobabble is a plague on the CSQ. When troubled parents come to me explaining away their angel's misbehavior by child development theories, I sigh, because I can predict those parent will be "DC"s, which, in the psychology biz, means 'Difficult Customers'! Some miseducation comes to us through familiar old wives' tales. However, today parents seem able to employ at least a little healthy skepticism about rules of child rearing passed down through generations. Unlike old wives' tales, however, psychobabble is insidious because often it is advice given by believable and trusted professionals who espouse theories about children which are presented as truths. Scientists know that all theories are based upon assumption and that a theory is not to be taken as a fact until a true cause and effect relationship has been proved. Unfortunately, too few parents share this understanding. We can be unwittingly victimized by well-meaning professionals who prescribe parenting rules according to child development theory, many of which *fly* in the face of common-sense. I sigh because earnest young parents, eager to be careful with a child's psyche, absorb psychobabble like berry juice on white muslin..so easy in, but so tough out! From my observations, psychobabble causes such a reduction in CSQ that I have hung this limerick in my office *for* parents:

EAT YOUR PEAS TO GET YOUR PIE!
REMEMBER THAT OLD SAW?
PLEASE, NO PSYCHOBABBLE,
JUST STICK WITH GRANDMA'S LAW.

Study the following vignettes and reflect on theories offered to you as advice. Be a healthy skeptic and decide whether *your* CSQ is under assault. Please note that every example is a true vignette although the child's name is false.

ARTHUR

Arthur, age 5, is abusive to his mother, single and divorced since Arthur was two years old. Arthur hits, snarls and commands his, mother to do his bidding and attend to him at whim. Arthur's play therapist tells mother to let Arthur vent his anger at her, because it reflects 'pre-verbal rage' about the divorce. This must not be allowed to fester, following the 'catharsis' theory that anger will disappear if allowed to be vented.

CSQ Skepticism: Who says an angry five year old is suffering from 'pre-verbal rage'? And where is the proof that venting anger at people solves problems? It might make one feel better for awhile, but does the problem disappear? Could not his anger simply reflect a childish G.I. disappointment?

CSQ Advice: Quickly, kindly, but firmly remove Arthur

to a time-out place as soon as he starts to attack his mother verbally or physically. Tell him he can choose to feel badly, but he must not do it all over other people. If he trashes his room while raging in time-out, that is his choice, but he will be expected to clean up the mess before he returns. Later Arthur and mother can discuss what is making Arthur angry and decide if it makes sense and how to solve the problem.

ALEX

Four-year-old Alex is playing among other pre-kindergarten children, and he throws a wooden block, narrowly missing another child. Based upon a theory that a four year old is not 'ready' to be held accountable for his unsociable behavior because he lacks complex evaluation skills, the teacher apologizes to Alex. She explains that she should have prevented him from his act, and thus she has caused Alex to experience fear when he realizes that he has nearly hurt another child.

CSQ Skepticism: Poppycock! That response is too confusing and delays simple but necessary training in socialization.

CSQ Advice: Quickly, kindly, but firmly remove Alex from the group. Tell him directly that he may not throw blocks because it hurts people. Tell him to sit on a chair for a few minutes, until the teacher comes back, and then be ready to 'tell the rule' about playing with blocks. After that Alex may return and show the teacher how he can play with blocks in a safe way. CSQ dictates that even though a child may be too young to evaluate fully the outcome of his impulsive behavior, the training should be enforced, kindly but firmly. Think about it from a common sense perspective. Do not parents talk to their babies long before their angels can understand the message? Of course, and they talk to their Alex because that is precisely how he 'gets ready' to develop language understanding. Readiness may require some necessary degree of physical development, but readiness is also influenced and shaped by training experience.

ASHLEY

Ashley, age five, insists she is afraid to sleep alone in her room. Mother has been influenced by several theories. Having been warned about Freud's theory of psycho-sexual stages of development, she does not dare to let Ashley sleep in the adults' bed. Her pediatrician, influenced by a different theory, advised her to pull a mattress into her daughter's room and sleep there so Ashley will not feel afraid. He tells mother that this is necessary in order to establish trust with a child, because if a child feels afraid and abandoned in early years, "she will not trust you at age 16." Mother obeys, without question, sleeping on a mattress every night in Ashley's room for the next two years. Every time Mother has tried to alter this condition, Ashley objects and cries that she is still afraid. So mother continues, hoping to ensure trust in adolescence.

CSQ Skepticism: This sounds crazy. You are teaching Ashley how to be manipulative and probably strengthening a childish phobia.

CSQ Advice: The very first time Ashley is afraid, listen carefully to her, and tell her there is a problem to be resolved. The first step is for both of you to decide whether there truly is a dangerous creature lurking in the night, or whether Ashley has a wonderful imagination that can create monsters from dark shadows. Explain to Ashley that if a real creature could be there, you would protect her from harm. However, imaginary creatures require a different program, and you will help her think up many tricks to chase away the imaginary monsters, such as: closing the shades at night to block out shadowy trees that might stir up scary visions; leaving a night light on for Ashley, keeping a ghost-buster ray gun handy for her to zap away any monster her imagination creates; rehearsing a dialogue Ashley could use to turn an ugly monster into a friendly creature; establishing a "Brave Star Chart" to mark and reward every night Ashley practices staying brave and handling the problem herself, even though she feels afraid. These interventions promote strength and common-sense in your angel, teaching her early steps in discriminating between real and irrational fears and without accidentally encouraging manipulative behavior.

ALBERT

Albert, age 10, misbehaves. He won't obey his parents and has been consistently smart-mouthing them. In fact, lately he has even taken to calling them names. Albert's

> *parents are worried and seek help from a professional who tells them that misbehavior simply reflects some developmental stage and is to be endured until it corrects itself. The parents are told, "Do nothing, ignore it and don't worry about it as long as the misbehavior occurs only at home. If Albert misbehaves like that outside of the home, then it is time to worry."*

CSQ Skepticism: Why would anyone conclude that misbehavior at home should be tolerated? And why must misbehavior be explained away as a stage? Everyone has heard of those 'terrible twos' to be sure. But do toddlers misbehave because they are two, or possibly because at two, sensible parents are beginning to confront their angel's G.I. juices? CSQ predicts that unfettered 'terrible twos' only become more terrible threes!

CSQ Advice: Teaching respect for others is a developmental task that must start early and start at home, among family members. Home is the easiest place to identify a bad habit in the making and to take a fast, kind but firm response, so that Albert learns by consequence training. Good manners taught at home will then generalize into the community, not the other way around. If you let you angel abuse you, you can expect it to continue. Follow the guidelines of EXPLAIN, TRAIN, REMAIN and REFRAIN.

Hopefully, you can understand why I say, "psychobabble makes me sigh."

CSQ AND CRAZY QUESTIONS

Remember that expression, 'ask a foolish question and you'll get a foolish reply'? I just bet that statement was written about parents. Not only do parents fall victim to psychobabble, but we seem to insist upon bombarding our misbehaving angel with foolish questions. Probably the all-time worst question is "WHY DID YOU DO THAT?" Foolish because you already know the true answer, which could only be, "BECAUSE I WANTED TO," and foolish because your wary child is bound to answer, instead, "I DON'T KNOW," Maybe you have already figured out that "I don't know" is a kid's version of the fifth amendment. Oh, a few may try to hold out with "I didn't do it" or "It wasn't my fault... he made me do it!" But most of the time your angel can cover the bases pretty well with, "I DON'T KNOW."

Let me save you tons of frustration. Here is a list of the most popular silly questions which you may feel duty bound to ask your angel when he misbehaves. Don't bother. They are not useful and probably won't bring you anything but exasperation. If you can train yourself to avoid confronting your angel with these questions, you might save a few points on your CSQ.

FOOLISH QUESTION REPLY	CHILD'S PROBABLE	TRUE ANSWER
Who did this?	... Not me!	... (I did, of course.)
Why did you do that?	... I don't know.	... (Because I wanted to.)

Surely you were not going to... were you?	... No, of course not!	... (Actually, I was!)
How could you do such a thing?	... I don't know.	... (It was easy.)
Where was your sense?	... I don't know.	... (I don't have any yet.)
How many times have I told you?	... I don't know.	... (Too many. I don't listen anymore.)
What is the matter with you?	... I don't know.	.. (Nothing.... I'm a kid.)
What made you do that?	... I don't know.	... (My GIMMEES and LEMMEES.)
Didn't you know what you were doing?	... I don't know.	... (Not really. Knowing means 'thinking about.')

I guess you get the idea. No learning takes place with those questions, for your child, except maybe how to stonewall effectively. Now I'm not against questions, just foolish ones. Good questions encourage a child to 'think about' his behavior, to verbalize a commitment to do things differently, to problem solve, and to own responsibility for his misbehavior. In general, try to follow this guide: stop asking WHO and WHY questions and switch to WHAT and HOW TO questions. Do not search for reasons, search for solutions to the problem your child has created for himself. Insist on a new plan and on a verbal commitment. And one last common-sense consideration! NEVER let questions, even good ones, substitute for a training consequence. Carry out a dialogue with your child only after the consequence has been completed.

Here are samples of useful questions to discuss with your angel that will help to raise his CSQ as well as yours:

What am I saying? Tell me in your own words.

What am I expecting you to do?

What might you do differently next time?
How will you make that happen?

What can you do now about this problem
you have created?

How does this make sense to you?
If you can't tell me, we'll try again.

What are your choices? Are you clear about them?

Will you choose, or shall I choose for you?

How will we know if you mean what you say?

By what time can I count on you to finish that job?

What do you think would be fair?
... Will it be fair for the rest of us?

How could you change to make it fair for all of us?

What can you expect to have happen
if you do this again?

How might we get you to 'think ahead'
the next time?

COMMON -SENSE SUMMARY

Common-sense includes the ability to assess conditions accurately yet flexibly and to plan wisely, in consideration of probable consequences. Children are notoriously poor at that. As a rule of thumb, the younger the child, the lower his CSQ... except for the aberrational period called adolescence, during which common-sense, in deference to raging hormones, seems to bottom out completely.

Raising children to 'grow up good' must include trying to program them to acquire common-sense, since a CSQ doesn't equate entirely with intelligence, and doesn't prove to develop magically on its own. Two ingredients seem essential in promoting a high CSQ in your child. Foremost, deliberately provide your child with plenty of practice in assessing conditions and choosing among alternatives about how to behave, and then let him experience reality consequences that follow those choices. Secondly, raise your own parental CSQ so you are free and able to carry out that strategy.

This chapter described several pitfalls to avoid which commonly lower parental CSQ. Be mindful of GIMMEE-IDONWANNA conflicts between your own GIs and your angel's motivation juices. Remember that the short-term avoidance of hassles (the 'easy' way out) usually proves to be more troublesome in the long run. And if you sense that your own GIs put you in constant power struggles with your child, check inward to decide if your own Triple-M might not need an overhaul.

Watch out for overdose POISON-PILLS which can include overprotection, overintrusion, overspecialing and overattachment. Poison-pill parenting usually results from irrational ideas you hold about your child's psyche and how it develops, and unfortunately, paradoxical results often occur. Overprotect your child and he becomes fearful; overspecial him and he becomes entitled; overcontrol or overintrude and he becomes stubborn, resistant or sneaky; overexplain and he quits listening; overcriticize and he becomes discouraged or vengeful; oversupervise and he becomes a passive non-thinker.

Keep a healthy skepticism of psychobabble! Don't be afraid to question a professional who espouses child-rearing theories as if they were factual laws of behavior and presumes to assign, explain and interpret symbolic meaning to a child's misbehavior. And if a problem behavior does not alter significantly after a short-term intervention, change the helper and the approach. Select only a professional helper with a reputation for having a high CSQ, not merely a wall full of diplomas. Avoid foolish questions when you confront your angel about his misbehavior. Change WHO and WHY questions to WHAT and HOW questions. Silly questions have no useful purpose because they do not stop misbehavior, nor promote common-sense. Common-sense questions, on the other hand, set up the opportunity for your Alex, Ashley or Andy to think differently, to problem solve and to own responsibility for their behavior.

Developing common-sense in your child requires courage. It is not easy for a parent to allow a child to make mistakes. But really, what is the alternative, in the long run? Keep trust in your child... not trust that he will never goof, lie or trick you. At times, he will. But trust that if you remain kind, firm and reality based, your child will survive the consequences of his choices and will learn from the real world rules of behavior. Discriminate the occasional boulders, which require you to shield your child, from the hundreds of pebble experiences which allow him to gain common-sense wisdom.

NORMA'S NUGGET:

WANT YOUR CHILD TO DEVELOP COMMON SENSE? THEN START WITH YOURSELF. CHECK OUT YOUR OWN CSQ.

Chapter 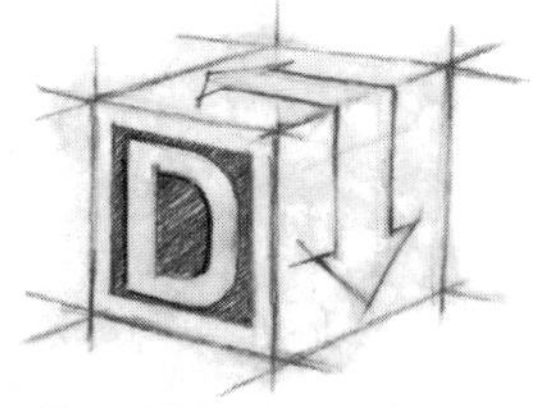

DOWN WITH DEMOCRACY

... Democracy applied to childrearing is often a souffle ideal with a pancake outcome.

I tried it, I really did. And then I tried it over and over again, so sure that it should work. But it just wouldn't. I'm talking about an idealized version of democracy and 'growin' up good.' Now don't get me wrong... I love democracy. I believe in it, and I always strived to extend it to my five children as they were growing. To me, democracy transcribes into some combination of freedom plus fairness and it seemed right that somehow those ingredients should fit smoothly into the pattern of good parenting. Democratic parenting was particularly appealing to me because I was raised in an authoritarian family. What I learned best as a child was how to obey, how to please others and how to avoid confrontation at any cost. In those days maybe 'cleanliness' was thought second to 'Godliness,' but surely 'obedience' ran a close third. Many generations ago that was the popular way to raise children. Every decision was easy. My parents' word was IT. Period. Expressions abounded such as 'children should be seen and not heard' and no adult had to fall back on the phrase 'end of discussion' because there was no discussion! A child's view didn't count. What he wanted didn't get a vote because a child was thought not to know what was 'best for him' and the idea that a child had rights was not a viable concept.

In the last few generations, the pendulum gradually swung in the opposite direction and parents began to consider their children as equal to adults... equal to pursue pleasures, equal not only in the right to have feelings and opinions but equal in the right to express them. Gone was the 'silent' child, replaced by a pretty mouthy one, allowed to opine all over the place. A child's 'wants' were redefined as 'needs,' angry outbursts considered a valid expression of frustration. Somehow, too, freedom of expression was extended to include freedom of choice with the assumption that, granted freedom from overcoercion, our little ones would exercise wisdom. When my five were young I remember well one popular notion proffered by child experts. They predicted that, given a full array of food choices spread on a table, a child would select a balanced diet on his own. This theory of 'domestic democracy' sounded wonderful to me, particularly in light of my children's finicky eating habits. (How vividly I recall an urgent, odoriferous, search when my daughter had stuffed cabbage down a hole in the kitchen wall!) So, filled with hopeful expectation, I tried the child-selection experiment. I can remember watching my children choose freely from an array of veggies, fruits, meats, grains and desserts. Guess what happened? Never once did a single child choose spinach or carrots over french fries or cookies. Never did a child ask for milk rather than cola. Never once did a child of mine select an apple over a candy bar. Not the first day, nor the second, nor any day for as long as I was able to endure the experiment. So much for the doctrine of 'domestic democracy'! Back we went to culinary common-sense with Grandma's Law... "eat your peas, then you'll get your pie." And I closed off that hole in my kitchen wall.

The big food fizz was not my only experiment with full democracy, but I must tell you that every attempt kept giving me little bits of unsettling feedback from my kids, nudging me back to authoritarian ways. My oldest son Billy educated me about the concept of power. Now I hated the idea that a parent would need to coerce a child by using brute power as a weapon. Such an undemocratic concept just goes against my nature. But one day twelve-year-old Billy came through the living room and dropped his coat on the floor. His Dad looked up and commanded, "Get your coat off the floor, pronto!" And Billy did, pronto. Boy, was I impressed! With some chagrin, I asked Billy how it was that I could not gain that rapid response? Was I not entitled to the same respect? Billy grinned, "Mom, what a silly question! Look in the mirror. What could you do to me, you little thing?"

Son Tony gave me another jolt about domestic democracy. One time he falsely confessed to writing a note in school, taking the blame instead of the real culprit. Naturally, I was perplexed and inquired about his false confession. He explained, "Because if Pete got into trouble his parents would have grounded him for life. We figured you would be much more reasonable, so I pretended I wrote the note." See what I mean? There is a real down side to being a democratic, understanding parent. That's one of the lessons I learned. Another was accepting a basic inequity built into parenting... big, strong fathers have it made... all they need to know is how to growl! But the rest of us lightweights need some other tools, like creative brains, if we are determined to remain even modestly democratic. So I began to think strategically and by the time my kids were teenagers I finally had begun to smarten up. For example, one time I couldn't get my sons to quit using my special lemon shampoo once they discovered girls and the value of showering... never mind that I bought them a giant supply of whatever product they wanted. It seemed that every time I reached for my lemon shampoo the bottle was empty. Attempts to hide it proved futile, appeals for fairness and consideration went for naught. Once again, so much for domestic democracy. So I used my brain. I poured my lemon shampoo into an empty physician's vial and pasted on a label, URINE SAMPLE. Just like magic! I could leave the vial anywhere I pleased and nobody bothered my shampoo again.

So what is the lesson to be learned? Should a parent become a tricky dissembler, full of deception and manipulation? Or, go back to an old authoritarian model of ruling by power and fear? No, of course not. The cost in the long run is too dear. Despite my occasional ventures into humorous dissembling, I recommend that you use such a strategy very sparingly and only in cases of self-preservation. Parents who habitually control their child through deception are really into subtle coercion, showing little respect for another person. If you make a habit of deception, your little one catches on to you eventually, and he begins to trick in return, or joins that stubborn game of "I gotcha!" Worse yet, most children raised solely by authoritarian power learn, as I did, to obey, how to please others and how to avoid confrontation, but they tend to do so indiscriminately, even when a specific situation might better suggest valid defiance. In fact, cult followers and habitually abused spouses often were children who grew into adults unable to recognize outrageous coercion, with little sense of power or self-worth. They can't seem to reap the benefits of democratic thinking because they never had adequate opportunities to make independent decisions, to run risks, to gain experiences out from under an ever present ominous shadow of recrimination.

THE SOLUTION

So what to do? Don't worry, I hit upon a good solution. I gradually figured out that you can't just start off with 100% domestic democracy right from the start. Kids can't handle it, because a democracy entails not just freedom, but freedom with responsibility, a sense of fairness and an ability to choose wisely. Choosing wisely involves self-discipline, long-term planning and sustained motivation. And it takes practice. So you had better start off authoritarian but loving. Loving in that you cherish your child and talk kindly to him, but authoritarian because you recognize that his GIMMEES and I DONWANNAS clash constantly with your wisdom and concern for his best interest. If you are a man with a big voice you have it easy. All you need to do is growl. If you are a light weight like me, follow the Teddy Roosevelt rule: Talk softly and carry a big stick—the big stick being clear thinking and firm action. Hang in resolutely with the following simple guidelines about WHO DECIDES WHAT between parent and child. It is a fool-proof system which will protect your child from the pitfalls of his underdeveloped self discipline, yet gives him enormous freedom to feel powerful and to practice decision making.

This is how the guidelines work. Reserve and declare three areas of decision-making as totally, 100% authoritarian. Make no apology about them, do not feel guilty and allow absolutely no discussion. Explain your rule (once only, and remember, do not confuse explaining with negotiating!) This is where you fit in the soft talk and big stick. List three areas on a chart under the heading DOWN WITH DEMOCRACY:

PERSONAL SAFETY DECISIONS
No child gets to vote on whether he can wander around the swimming pool without a vest, for instance. In my family no child could obtain permission to ride or buy a motorcycle. These are just examples, of course. The important point is that if the topic is personal safety, the child does not get a vote, nor does the parent open the topic for negotiating.

PLAYING FAIR DECISIONS
No child gets to vote on whether he is allowed to walk on the rights of anyone else, whether it be parents, sibs, housekeepers, pets, friends, etc. No matter what the age of the child, all behaviors that violate rights of others must be interrupted and stopped, immediately. Very often parents stop older sibs from bullying or tricking younger ones, but do not notice how they allow a young child to intrude on the rights of an older sib or on adults. Even if the child is too young to understand "why," he is to be stopped. Not

punished, but stopped, pronto. He will come to understand, gradually, about the rights and feelings of others. And consider not what the child declares as fair. He gets no vote nor free speech. The important point is that there is no room for negotiation. Down with democracy! Insist that your child act in fairness, no matter if he does not agree.

PERSONAL RESPONSIBILITY DECISIONS

This category includes those behaviors which train a child to develop good work habits, a sense of commitment and responsibility. These would include doing homework, for example, which is unrelated to physical safety or rights of others but promotes self-discipline, as do attending to chores, brushing teeth, getting to school on time. All of these develop personal responsibility. If your child wanted to have a small part-time job and he signed to do it, then there should be no room for negotiation a month later when he is tired of the task. A reasonable amount of carry-through time is to be insisted upon. So also with joining a sports team; signing up for a series of lessons. A reasonable commitment of time would be obvious, such as the end of the sport season, and the commitment must include a good effort at practice and attendance. Down with Democracy here.

The parent decides if a behavior fits one of these three categories. If it does, no discussion. The child gets no vote. Sounds terribly autocratic, and it is. However, the guideline excludes every other decision, leaving to the child many, many opportunities to choose and decide for himself about meaningful events. For example, the child gets to choose his clothes on most occasions, no matter how ghastly the combination. How he spends his allowance is his choice, although a parent might veto too much candy as a violation of health and safety.

Following this simple guideline is not always as easy as you might think. If you monitor your own behaviors honestly and carefully, you might be surprised to discover how unnecessarily intrusive you tend to be. I remember one family that was ensnared in power struggles and in this case the parents were not playing fair. Their teenage daughter was allowed to drive the family car, on occasion, but only after she lost five pounds, changed her wardrobe to her mother's satisfaction and altered her hair style. To this program I cried "FOUL" because none of those decisions fit into any of the three categories listed. Try to play fair and keep this distinction clear: your child should be free to question whether a choice fits within the guidelines... that is fair and democratic, but if the behavior does fit, DOWN WITH DEMOCRACY for that situation.

DOMESTIC DEMOCRACY: NO PLAN C

I guess by now you know that I really do believe in giving children choices. If you will hold firm on those three sacred categories, you can remain a sensibly democratic parent, and you can do that by understanding 'NO PLAN

C.' Have you heard about PLAN C? PLAN C means a behavior your child is not allowed to choose, because it violates one of those sacred categories. Instead, you offer Alex reasonable alternatives from which he does get to choose, which I call PLAN A or PLAN B. Suppose, for example, Alex wants to eat a popsicle in the living room while he is watching TV. Mother says "No" (category 2... it violates her rights if sticky, colored water drips on her rug). Alex could try to negotiate and promise not to drip his popsicle or promise to eat it over a plate, but any experienced mother knows that is not a viable option... time for that firm refusal. However, she could allow her child to save face, to feel empowered, and still experience an opportunity to make choices if she will tell him, "You can choose to eat a popsicle in the kitchen, then come into the living room to watch TV (PLAN A) or you can save the popsicle for later and stay in the living room now to watch TV (PLAN B) but you can't eat the popsicle in the living room" (NO PLAN C). Count on it... given the opportunity, every Alex, Ashley and Andy will try to hold out for PLAN C, using negotiation, complaint, wheedling, delay, or any other tactic designed to back you down. Remember the firm rule: NO DISCUSSION, NO TACTICS. If the child stalls without selecting PLAN A or PLAN B, stay pleasant, wait only a short, reasonable time, tell him he can still choose immediately, or you will have to choose for him this time. Then do so, remaining pleasant, firm but action determined. Often a child will test you, and pretend to choose a plan, such as, "OK, I'll eat the popsicle in the kitchen" but in just a few minutes, you will notice that Alex has inched his way into the living room, still eating his popsicle. If he is allowed to continue, perhaps because Mom is too busy to deal with him or just doesn't want a confrontation over what seems like such a little deal, Mom is making a mistake. While the particular event might not be a big deal, the training lesson is. If Mom does not follow through with distinguishing PLANS A or B from NO PLAN C, Alex has not merely eaten a popsicle in the living room, he has learned how to be manipulative, a much larger problem than a popsicle on the rug. In this situation, Mom would best turn off the TV, put Alex back in the kitchen and declare the opportunity lost for this occasion. If Alex says, "No, no, I'll stay in the kitchen and then watch TV," Mom needs to say, "No, not today. Tomorrow you can choose again." And not let him back to TV even when his popsicle is finished! Otherwise, Alex learns to think, "Oh, well, nothing ventured, nothing gained... it was worth a try, since my gamble didn't really cost me anything."

You will be surprised how often you can allow your child plenty of choices between PLANS A or B, but not C. Gradually your angel learns to think ahead and to practice choosing among socially acceptable alternatives that do not compromise his safety, his responsibility training, nor violate the rights of others, which is really what 'growin' up good' is all about.

NORMA'S NUGGETS:

LET YOUR CHILD CHOOSE BETWEEN PLAN A OR B... BUT NO PLAN C! PLAY FAIR... BUT DO NOT SEEK PERMISSION NOR EXPECT CONSENSUS FROM YOUR CHILD.

Chapter E

ENTITLEMENT - YOUR ROYAL I'NESS

... Unfortunately, when a too precious person falls in love, it is with himself. Worse yet, he proves to be monogamous.

If your child is three or four years old, can he pass the telephone test? I don't mean if he knows his phone number or can answer the telephone properly. I am not referring to HIS telephone test, but YOURS. Does he pass YOUR telephone test? And do you? It goes like this: you wish to chat with a friend on the phone for a few minutes, without interruption, and you politely request your Ashley to leave you alone for just a brief time. But, despite your request, Ashley seems to develop a sudden, urgent need for your attention and interrupts you so frequently that you abandon your phone conversation.

Does your child allow you this short freedom without turning into that pesky, persistent mosquito? And you? Do you insist on your rights? Be honest. If your answer is NO, beware! You might be observing an early indication of that dreadful developmental disorder I call ENTITLEMENT: YOUR ROYAL I'NESS.

What do I mean by Entitlement? Entitlement is a set of childishly unrealistic perceptions of self-importance, which negatively affects how a too precious person relates to others. Entitlement can be conceptualized as a developmental problem in socialization. During the first two or three years of life infants and toddlers have a very limited and self-centered concept of other persons, their earliest interactions leading them to believe that others exist solely to provide safety, comfort and pleasure. The new child is the center of the family universe. He is truly precious and helpless, and parents gladly suffer all demands. From the start we teach an infant, "You are special... our love for you is total and non-contingent... we will always love you, no matter what." Now everybody knows that this is a great way to nurture your baby, psychologically, in his early years. So by age three, Andy, Alex and Ashley have a rhyme in their heads that goes like this:

I am very important, very precious and special.
How do I know?
Because from the day I arrived
You have told me so!

What is not so obvious to children is the essential sequel to their infantile perception which goes: "Even though we love you freely, you must learn that other people exist, and that eventually they will love you only if you play fair, be caring and helpful, even when you are being inconvenienced. You are important, of course, but so is everyone else."

So we seem to have a paradox. The seeds of Entitlement are planted naturally in the early years by loving parents, and yet what starts off so right can actually turn harmful, becoming one of those 'poison pills' described earlier. If you declare your child too precious, overindulging him with attention, your little one comes to believe he is entitled to and thus owed a constant one-on-one relationship with a doting, attentive adult. Then, if such devotion continues beyond toddlerhood without some beginning insistence upon reciprocity, the stage is set for Entitlement. So, we might say that, from the start, socialization seems to require a correction factor, especially because gentle parents tend to assume that modeling selfless, giving behavior will guarantee a well-socialized youngster. Modeling is probably crucial, but proves insufficient. Moderation and reciprocity are equally important ingredients, moderation in indulgences and insistence upon some age-appropriate reciprocity.

Even wise parents are commonly lulled into ignoring the reciprocity principle because they assume that it is unfair to expect a child to demonstrate social skills beyond his conceptual awareness. That seems logical and yet... would you decide not to chatter at your baby because your little one does not yet have language skills and therefore cannot be expected to respond? Of course not! In fact, the more you talk at a baby, long before expecting any reply, the more you are shaping his language. The same principle extends to social training. Using only a gentle manner, without recourse to scolding or condemning, you can begin to insist that even a toddler allow you and other family members to enjoy a few pleasures of your own, no matter if inconvenient to your baby Royal I'Ness, and no matter if he does not yet 'understand.' The experiencing is how he gradually comes to understand.

So, you see, Royal I'Ness status becomes firmly established quite naturally and therefore, needs to be kindly, but equally firmly, dethroned. The GOOD NEWS is that early Entitlement can be described as no more than a delay in social-emotional development, still easy to correct. At this stage, a child of Entitlement is not a case of 'growin' up bad' but merely 'not growin' up... yet.' The BAD NEWS is that the longer the Entitlement grows and firms, the more difficult to restrain or eliminate. By adolescence uncorrected Entitlement no longer qualifies as merely a developmental delay, in my opinion, but becomes a developmental disorder, highly resistant to remediation, and by young adulthood almost impossible to reverse. I call this encroaching developmental disorder the GIMMEE-PIG syndrome.

ABOUT GIMMEE-PIGS

A Royal I'Ness condition begins to fit the GIMMEE-PIG syndrome after a child's GIMMEEs and LEMMEEs long outrun realistic rules of the world. We all know GIMMEE-PIGS when we meet them. At least I do... and when I happen upon one, I run in the opposite direction! They are people who, given an inch, immediately go for that mile. But did you know that GIMMEE-PIGS have formulated a well defined social doctrine? It runs like this:

GIMMEE-PIG Proclamation: "All the cookies belong to me..."

GIMMEE-PIG Logic: "... because I REALLY want them, don't you see?"

GIMMEE-PIG Rule #1: "If I REALLY want them, I should have them!"

GIMMEE-PIG Rule #2: "Since I should have them, YOU should give them."

Think of some GIMMEE-PIGS you know beyond age four. See if they match the description of Entrenched Entitlement:

- The Entitled Child looks, sounds and acts like a GIMMEE-PIG. Offer him one cookie and he demands two. He confuses SOME with MORE. Give him some and he demands more.
- The Entitled Child declares himself equal to an adult in asserting his 'rights' and expressing his opinions, no matter when or where. He believes he is always owed an explanation and if he doesn't like the message, he is owed bargaining rights.
- The Entitled Child confuses the distinction between PRIVILEGES and RIGHTS. He believes a privilege becomes a right if he wants some pleasure strongly enough. ("But Dad, you don't understand... I REALLY, REALLY want it.")
- The Entitled Child confuses a REQUEST with a DEMAND. He believes that a request stated in a pleasant voice should be honored. ("But Dad, I asked *politely* for the car, so how come I still can't have it?")

- The Entitled Child truly believes he is owed pleasures and freedom from hassle as a natural birthright. He has a low frustration tolerance and is quick to anger because he believes he should not be forced to experience discomfort.
- The Entitled Child believes others owe him happiness. ("My brother is supposed to help me... my teacher is supposed to understand me... my mother is supposed to drive me around.") An older child of Entitlement frequently prefaces his statements with "I deserve... I resent... It's not fair... You are supposed to... " He is a master at expressing anger and resentment and in attempts to lay guilt trips on those who refuse his demands.
- The Entitled Child notoriously lacks a sense of appreciation, seldom expressing gratitude. This habit is not surprising since he perceives his 'wants' as 'rights.'
- The Entitled Child has limited empathy. He has little sense of true equality, kindness or fairness, because he does not perceive other persons as equally precious. He is not cruel and does not intend to hurt others. He can show concern for another, but only so long as his generosity does not cost him personal discomfort. He considers himself pleasant and interesting, so he believes that bestowing himself is a gift to others. Thus he is bewildered and quick to anger if he is not considered special by everyone.

If you could hear the thoughts of an Entitled Child, they would sound like this:

> *I am equal to an adult and I own you. You are supposed to care about me, keep me happy... in fact, I provide your most important purpose in life. I am your Royal I'Ness and you are my servant. I command you to tell me I am special and wonderful, to play with me and stay with me, one-on-one. Under no circumstances may you ignore me or share yourself with anyone else if that excludes me. I will grant you a few privileges providing they don't cost me inconvenience and as long as you obey my commands I will remain pleasant. I am the most important person. I am entitled to a life of pleasure and comfort, without hassle and with little effort. As my parent, your job is to provide all of this for me. In return, I will pleasure you by existing.*

In sum, the problem with Entitlement is not merely a case of GIMMEE-PIG demanding, but rather a distortion in perception. Expectations are unrealistic. Entitled Andy truly believes his fair share is both cookies on the plate, assumes that others exist to make him happy, and firmly expects devotion. As a result of this distorted perspective, he is frequently angry, perceiving even essentially fair treatment as unfair. Entitlement is not limited to childhood, of course. A history of previous experiences will set the stage for Entitlement, no matter the age. Ponder this:

Chapter E

Suppose a generous employer hired you for $50 an hour to perform work that ordinarily pays $20 per hour and has allowed you to arrive late, go home early and take unlimited days off. After years of this idyllic but unrealistic circumstance your employer learns that his expenses are threatening his business. So he tightens the rules and announces that now you can earn only $30 per hour (still above the going rate), must arrive on time, stay productive for a full eight hours and take only a limited number of personal days.

How would you feel? (Be honest!) Predictably, you would feel resentful, despite the reality that the new working conditions remain fair, even generous. The true problem is not the 'unfairness' of your employer, but the unrealistic expectations which your employer allowed you to experience. The dilemma is always in the misperception of 'fairness' as erroneously measured by the Entitled person.

In my office I listen to Entitled adolescents who express resentment when their parents balk at paying for designer clothes. They feel abused and cheated by a parent who pays 100% of the adolescent's auto insurance but tries to limit use of the family car to one night per weekend. Says the angry GIMMEE-PIG, "If I can have the car for one night, why not two? You stay home anyway! You might as well never give it to me! You don't even care if I can't do the same things as all my friends. You are not fair." And he believes himself.

I wish I could tell you that these observations are rare

occurrences, limited only to professional cases... but not so. Here is a true, unembellished vignette of a seven year old Entitled GIMMEE-PIG whom I was unlucky enough to encounter just recently in a suburban dress shop:

> *As I was perusing, I heard a seven-year-old Ashley assault her mother. Apparently, the child had asked for a new red dress she had admired, but Mother had said, "no, not today." Thereupon Ashley began to tantrum. "I want the red dress. I REALLY want it. I don't want it just a little, I want it a LOT. Don't you hear me? I hate you! You are a mean, rotten mother!" Ashley stomped and wailed a full five minutes, unabated. Customers, myself included, shrank away, embarrassed. Mother calmly ignored Ashley until the child finally paused, perhaps to rest a moment from her tirade. Immediately Mother spoke sweetly and invited the child to give an opinion between two dresses Mother was considering for herself, sort of a buddy-buddy dialogue between two rational adults. Ashley looked briefly, scornfully pronounced her choice and immediately added, "Well, I see you are buying yourself a new dress. If you get one, I should too. So will you buy me the red dress?" To my dismay, Mother replied, "Well, it depends. Will you promise not to ask for anything else today if I buy it for you?" Next Ashley became irritated. "Yes, of course. I already*

> *told you I don't want anything but this red dress!" Mother capitulated. "Well, alright. I guess that sounds fair. We'll buy this one for me and the red one for you."*

And that is a GIMMEE-PIG Child of Entitlement... just in case you missed the diagnosis. Will Ashley keep her promise and ask for nothing more? Of course not. How long will she remain pleasant? Exactly until her eyes light upon another potential GIMMEE pleasure. She may (or may not) give verbal thanks, but her appreciation will not carryover to her next enticement.

What was that mother doing? What could she have been thinking? I believe Mother thought she was responding appropriately by ignoring the tantrum. While ignoring misbehavior is often a good strategy, here it was the wrong time and place. She allowed her child to annoy everyone in the store for far too long. Instead of dealing directly with the child's infantile demands, Mother tried to distract her and elevated her to the status of an adult. Distraction, like ignoring, is useful when appropriate, but again this was the wrong time, wrong place. Mother might better have given Ashley one warning at the onset of the tantrum, and then, if not heeded, have driven her home immediately. Mother would then return to shop alone as soon as possible, making clear why Ashley may not accompany her. Ashley had gained no valuable experience in learning that other people's rights were being violated. Probably Mother thought she was teaching Ashley to compromise by settling only for a dress. She wasn't. In truth, Mother was programming a long-term Entitled GIMMEE-PIG. Ashley's demandingness paid off, eventually, after a prolonged, inappropriate interaction.

The child did not learn that she was not entitled to a new dress just because her mother bought one for herself. Ashley's irrational belief that her request should be honored according to how greatly she wanted the dress was reinforced. Sadly, Ashley learned nothing except to underscore her already firm opinion that she is, indeed, a special and important Royal I'Ness.

Not every Child of Entitlement is identified by indulgences in GIMMEE-PIG pleasures. One more vignette describes a Child of Entitlement who was not overindulged in possessions, but in being granted special status as a too-precious person. I consider this type of Entitlement even more difficult to ameliorate:

> *Six-year-old Doug was about to achieve a remarkable feat just before I met him... being expelled from school after only two months in the first grade. He had a very superior IQ and could already read, so special adjustments allowed precocious Doug to work independently. Doug loved school, but his social behaviors were atrocious. He considered himself the class leader and expected other children to defer to him, which they did only some of the time. When they did not, he would become enraged. The crisis was that Doug had hit his teacher with his lunch box and waved scissors at her when she tried to approach him. Doug expressed contempt for his teacher, describing her as 'stupid and a liar.' His 'proof' of her stupidity was that she had failed to notice a mistake on his paper and*

he labeled her a liar because she told him she had eyes in the back of her head to see him if he acted naughty. I asked him why he was so angry at his teacher and he explained that if she scolds him the other children might laugh. Said he, "I am smarter than everyone else and smarter than my teacher so I don't need to listen to her. I hit her on purpose so everyone would know how big and smart I am."

When I interviewed Doug's parents, the basis for his Entitlement was evident. They were thrilled with their gifted child and made several references to how easily he learned and how much he loved school, so they were perplexed about his misbehavior. At home, however, they admitted that Doug was abusive to his elderly grandmother. He would play chess with her, but scream and call her names when she took too long or made a foolish move. When I asked Mother what consequence followed such an attack she said, "We always talk to him and explain that 'Grandmother is old and not as smart as you so you should be patient with her'."

These parents were attempting to appeal to Doug through reasoning, alone, assuming that a gifted intellect would automatically coincide with social and emotional maturity. Not so. They were measuring his maturity using only a cognitive yardstick. No one held Doug accountable for his rudeness and infantile grandiosity. He was considered so special and precious that he was allowed complete Royal I'Ness status at home, which in turn made trouble at school. Implicit in the handling of Doug with Grandmother was the message that he is a superior being because of his superior intellect and therefore he has a 'royal' obligation to be patient and kind to the rest of us inferior humans whose main purpose on earth is to help cultivate his precious specialness.

Unfortunate Doug. He was well on his way to Entrenched Entitlement. Of what relative importance that he could read before age six if he has so little awareness of himself as a social being? Might not even precocious children require consequences to promote self-discipline? Indeed they do and parents of talented children carry an extra burden in helping their child to internalize the crucial message that a superior skill does not equate to a superior being.

. . . "JUST BETWEEN ME AND YOU" . . .

Remember the telephone test? If your child has reached age four and has already acquired a sense of early Entitlement, get busy. Do not make the mistake of assuming that your angel will develop social skills by divine osmosis... some magical process by which social awareness will seep in passively. Home must provide the initial introduction to 'otherness' and 'fairness,' the first step in preventing Entitlement. The initial opportunity occurs not between siblings but between you and your child. In fact, insisting that your little one accommodate you, even just a little bit, is one of the best ways to prevent jealousy in an older child when a new baby arrives.

Send this message to your Royal I'Ness toddler that says:

**"I love you, your Royal I'Ness,
But just between me and you...
I count too!"**

Here are some small beginnings. Insist that your Andy, even as a toddler, waits just a bit when he demands a GIMMEE. Tell him, "Wait a minute. I am busy." ... or, "Not yet. It is my turn. Please wait." And having declared your equality, never let an ensuing tantrum deter your resolve. Insist that your four year old fill some empty time without demanding that you own the problem. Say, "Please find something to do by yourself." And then do not let him ignore your request. If he complains of boredom, let him either solve the problem or experience the boredom which is, after all, but a mild discomfort. Allow Ashley to experience some inevitable disappointment without distracting her or offering a consolation prize. Require her to remain quiet and to share you with a third person (or the telephone!) without interrupting or center-staging. If she persists with mosquito behavior remove her immediately from your presence... do not stop to explain or bargain or apologize... and be sure to finish your conversation without her.

Insist that your little one use the magic words 'please' and 'thank you' and that your child keep a respectful tone when talking to you. Do not let Ashley call you names, reproach you, attack you or demand explanations. Say, "I don't talk to you that way and I will not let you talk to me like that either." I cannot count the dozens of parents I see who feel helpless to confront their rude child. These parents appear embarrassed, they shake their heads, throw up their hands in defeat, as if to say, "This is a burden one must endure with children until they eventually outgrow this bad behavior." Poppycock! Allowing Andy to express an opinion in an appropriate way is reasonable, but you do not owe your child haranguing privileges. Let him know that he is 'tiring your ears' which is an infringement on your own rights. You do not need to be a helpless victim. Don't get resentful, get resolute. Remember DOWN WITH DEMOCRACY? Remember NO PLAN C? It fits right here. The next time your telephone rings, let your child decide if he wants to play quietly near you while you talk on the phone, or if he wants to play noisily somewhere else... but he cannot choose to stand by and harangue you. NO PLAN C!

FAMILY FARE (FAIR!)

We can recognize that confronting Early Entitlement starts between a parent and a child, one-to-one. Often, however, a family constellation includes more people trying to live together in harmony than just you and your single child. And unfortunately, if even one family member proves to be an Entrenched Royal I'Ness, everyone is affected negatively.

Siblings can be especially victimized, in need of protection. When I encounter a family trying to survive the ordeal of living with a GIMMEE-PIG, I gather all of them together, and announce OUT with the now familiar 'Telephone Test' and IN with what I call the 'Dog Dilemma' riddle, which goes like this:

"Pretend you have bought a new dog,

Ruff. Everyone is excited and happy. Unfortunately, Ruff is a biter. He bites everybody in the family no matter what you try. What must you do?"

Usually everyone readily agrees that the dog must be returned because everyone is being hurt and the home is not safe or fun for anyone. Then I continue:

"Now pretend that Ruff does not bite everyone ... not Mom or Dad, not Alex nor Ashley, but only Andy. Andy is not cruel to Ruff and does not tease him, but still Ruff just doesn't seem to like Andy. He growls and bites Andy, so Andy feels afraid and unhappy. What must you do?"

The answer, of course, remains that the dog must go. From this riddle emerges the guiding principle for parents to follow which I call FAMILY FARE. It states simply that all house rules and social interactions between family members must stand the test of SAFE, FAIR and RESPECTFUL for EVERY MEMBER. In the case of the dog, keeping Ruff would have violated SAFE and FAIR.

Of the three tenets, SAFE, FAIR and RESPECTFUL, children seem to have the most difficulty with the concept of FAIR, even when they do not qualify as a child of Entitlement... and for a true GIMMEE-PIG, FAIR becomes the red flag of demand. Most parents want to treat their children fairly, even overextending themselves as they attempt to guarantee equity. Implicit in the concept of 'loving and caring' is the intent to treat another fairly. The important nugget to remember from an earlier chapter is that all children remain self-centered for many years, and cannot be expected to reason beyond the lure of their particular GIMMEEs and IDONWANNAs. Therefore, you, the adult, must determine what is fair, not the child! Do not fall into the trap of thinking that your child must agree that you are being fair, or that you must compromise with your Royal I'Ness's version of fairness. Just be as fair as you can, according to your own common sense, no matter if the child disagrees.

Fairness between siblings is an ever-presenting problem for family counselors. Once again, of course, any two children being forced to share time, space and treasures will clash, being I-centered. Most professionals advise parents to stay removed from sibling squabbles, letting children work out problems for themselves. I would agree in general, but with a caveat. Certainly, tattley-tales and complaining should be discouraged, while cooperative endeavors be encouraged and rewarded. When my five children were getting old enough for me to leave them home without a conventional babysitter, I designed a contract that worked really well. The rules of behavior were clearly written and reviewed with everyone together, and then I told them they would be able to divide the money reserved for a sitter, the next morning, provided all five children agreed that everyone else had been fair and cooperative. Not once did any child complain! Heaven only knows, for sure, what they did in my absence, but I figured if they were all friendly and satisfied the next morning, I really didn't need to know all the details.

Now the caveat. Perhaps I was a wise parent, or perhaps I was merely a lucky one, for I had no GIMMEE-PIGs among my five children. I guide parents, however, that the decision to step in or nose out depends on the children involved. They key phrase is "It depends." A Child of Entitlement in a family plays by a different set of rules, and often sibs cannot stand up against a strong, demanding personality, no matter the age. Siblings of an entrenched GIMMEE-PIG need protection. Not infrequently I review a depressed, angry, older sib who is actually feeling frustrated and helpless because he is expected to be patient and understanding of a younger GIMMEE-PIG sibling. Perhaps the young bandit has been allowed continual access to the older child's room and his prized possessions, with little or no restraint, and no consequences. The older child is not allowed to take aggressive action and has no way to defend his rights, while the younger, Entitled Child quickly learns to take advantage. I have known older children required to retire early along with their younger sibs, for example, merely because the little gorilla will tantrum, and the parents want to avoid hassle.

More obvious, of course, is the protection for the younger sib from an older entrenched GIMMEE-PIG, who would habitually trick or bully without parental involvement. So you can understand why I add the caveat ... "it depends" ... when parents ask about refereeing squabbles.

Try to set the family stage for fairness to everyone, to a reasonable degree, without falling into the trap of orchestrating every family interaction. Fairness is an idealistic condition that is impossible to maintain in daily life, and children benefit from small doses of experiencing this disappointing reality, without recourse to self-pity, whining or revenge. On Andy's special occasions, such as his party or having a guest over night he should be allowed his 'specialness' without harassment or intrusion, and without compensation due to Alex or Ashley. They can be expected to help special Andy, with the reminder that they will get their turn too... but not today. Equality in fairness and fun does not need to be measured and balanced by the moment, as long as an Entrenched Royal I'Ness is not allowed to reign by terror.

What a difficult task is growing up! One might not realize that learning to cooperate and to acquiesce gracefully requires practice. A child who is reinforced in his expectation that the world OWES him total fairness is headed for misery.

A note about RESPECT in FAMILY FARE. Part of 'growin' up good' means that your child values the feelings and rights of others, no matter who the person, and that he conveys that message in his choice of words and tone as he communicates. Several times in this book I have reminded you that modeling kind and caring behavior toward your child is not sufficient as a training technique, but here, above all, is where parental modeling does truly count. If you insist that your little one talk and act respectfully to you but you command your child in an imperious manner, he will gradually come to feel shamed and unworthy, or feel hurt and become rebellious. Neither of these conditions augers well for 'growin' up good.' I cannot underscore enough the recommendation that while you remain firm you also remain kind and respectful of your child's feelings. You can insist that your child obey you without sounding like a marine drill sergeant. As you remain respectful in tone, you have set the stage to insist that Alex and Ashley and Andy follow your model and treat not only you but each other without rudeness. RESPECT starts with you.

In summary, you are your child's first, early teacher.

Here is where that proverbial 'ounce of prevention' is worth far more than that 'pound of cure.' So do not let a baby gorilla in your family grow into a Royal I'Ness of gargantuan proportions. But if, unfortunately, this warning is too late and you are already living with a full grown GIMMEE-PIG, don't despair. Read the Addendum Chapter. It will help you establish a structured program for declaring war on Entrenched Entitlement.

NORMA'S NUGGET:

REMEMBER THE RULE . . .YOUR ROYAL I'NESS, JUST BETWEEN ME AND YOU . . . I COUNT TOO!

Chapter 

FUZZY FEELINGS - *Find 'em, Face 'em, Fix 'em!*

... "I do NOT have thin skin, I just have thick feelings!"
... Unknown

One day five-year-old Andy came to me and asked, Grandma, what are feelings?" An innocent enough question, but you know, he had me stumped. I paused for a moment, and then realized I couldn't think how to explain to a young child about emotions... the assignment seemed too difficult. Just what are feelings, anyway? We might say feelings are nothing less than the 'stuff of life.' They present as a network of intrigue... so intricate, so nebulous, yet so powerful in how they affect us. Emotions steer our ship, determine our course of action, often dictating what we say and what we do. Feelings, with all their intensity and poignancy... love, hate, pride, shame, fear... wield such control over us. Would we want to eradicate emotions, we might ask? Certainly not. They motivate us, energize us and provide intangible pleasure in our lives. Feelings are the color and fabric of our existence, forging those bonds of intimacy connecting people which we so cherish and endlessly pursue.

Under ordinary circumstances, mature people behave purposefully, mostly making decisions with logic and foresight. A flood of emotions, however, can turn us from reasonable actors into emotional reactors. Plain and simple, emotions and reasoning are incompatible, the more of the former guaranteeing less of the latter. Remember that Common Sense Quotient in Chapter C? Fall in love ... instantly lose 100 points off your CSQ! Think of it another way. We practice fire drills when we are calm, hoping an automatic procedure will protect us from confusion under panic.

When dysfunctional people seek professional help, emotions always prove an important part of the equation... sometimes as overwhelming as an ocean wave, other times murky and elusive. Too much emotion triggers outbursts of troublesome behavior, while too little emotion limits intimacy. An emotionally constricted person defends against feeling emotional pain, resisting, denying, even to himself, an awareness of his feelings.

Children understand none of this. In fact, even adults seem to remain incredibly ignorant about emotions. Very few people I know can accurately recognize and articulate important feelings they experience, much less deal with them effectively.

Why does such ignorance exist? I have come to believe that people simply have not been educated adequately about feelings, often at an enormous psychological cost. We mistakenly believe that expressing feelings is a show of weakness, a vulnerability. Somehow we have come to believe that 'grown-up,' mature people do not emote. Babies show feelings, not adults! The discrimination lost to many of us is that maturity does not mean that we do not have or acknowledge feelings but rather that we manage them appropriately, that we take charge and guide our ship through emotional waters. Managing feelings does not equate with denying them. To the contrary, good management dictates that we become cognizant of our feelings, ever aware of their potential power, and skillful in our ability to experience, monitor and benefit from them.

Both children and adults need to make friends with the concept of feelings. Think back to our childhood education. We spent hundreds of school hours learning to precisely identify and label nouns, adjectives, verbs and conjunctions. But was any importance assigned to teaching us to identify and differentiate between the feelings of anger, fear, guilt, shame, jealousy? Teachers endlessly pounded into our heads the 'Rules of Grammar'... those vital connections between a noun and an adjective, between two clauses and a conjunction, but those teachers never taught us the 'Rules of Emotions'... how our feelings are directly connected to our thinking habits and early experiences. Yet which of these lessons carries more impact on the quality of our lives?

Since educators have not been given the responsibility to teach children fully about feelings, this chapter is addressed to you, the parent. Read carefully to fully grasp the vital hook-up between thoughts, feelings and behavior. Helping Alex, Ashley and Andy to understand this relationship is a major part of 'growin' up good,' so this chapter is all about feelings and has been divided into three separate conceptual assignments ... FINDING FEELINGS, FACING FEELINGS and then FIXING FEELINGS, when they present a problem.

FINDING FEELINGS

Babies have plenty of feelings, right from the start.

They first experience them from sensations—they see, hear, touch, smell and taste things, and their feelings are a direct response to their physical comfort or pain. Recalling Chapter A, babies are 100% happy or 100% not, and they shift from one mood to the other in what seems like only an instant. Babies definitely do not hide their emotions and *for* sure they know how to alert us when they are not happy! No, babies have no problem experiencing feelings; they face the developmental task of learning how to differentiate, specify and eventually to manage them.

Early on, babies begin to record their experiences as memories in their fantastic computer memory bank. As their brain cells mature they hook together experiences and memories, bringing about conceptual understanding but also the beginnings of automatic, conditioned emotional responses. Young children learn first to differentiate and express "I feel happy" and "I feel bad" but little else. They do not have much of a vocabulary for 'feeling' words so they can't articulate different feelings with precision and they can't match their feelings appropriately to specific events. Now you can't go on much of a detective hunt if you can't label what you are looking for. So, the major task in this first conceptual component is to help your child become aware of various feelings, learn to label them, and to match them appropriately to events. While your child is still a preschooler, try to stretch his conceptual and expressive vocabulary to include the four basic emotions: SAD... MAD... GLAD... and SCARED. That is an excellent starting goal. Share with him when you experience one of those feelings, personally. Talk about the words and more importantly, fit them into the context of an event. When reading the old, familiar bedtime stories for example, digress a bit to explore how the characters feel. Since certain situations tend to trigger specific feelings, help your child understand the hook-up. Ask, "How did Bambi feel when his mother died?" (SAD, SCARED); "How did the little pig feel when the wolf was blowing down his straw house?" (SCARED); "How did Mr. McGregor feel when Peter Rabbit ate his carrots?" (MAD) "How did the Prince feel when the glass slipper fit Cinderella?" (GLAD). Do this consistently so that your child begins to attend not only to the story action but to develop an awareness of the feelings experienced by the characters. Always let him know that feelings are natural and predictable.

A second step is to expand Alex, Ashley and Andy's 'feeling' vocabulary along three directions. First, enriching their vocabulary with simple synonyms:

glad = happy mad = angry scared = afraid

Second, differentiating intensities of the same feeling:

a little bit angry = irritated or annoyed,
BUT
very angry = furious or enraged

a little afraid = apprehensive or worried,
BUT
very fearful = panic or terror!

Third, conceptualizing additional emotions beyond the basic four. Building a 'feelings' vocabulary is a gradual process over several years. You cannot expect a preschooler or even a primary grade child to handle a word like 'apprehensive,' of course, but by ages 8 - 10 Alex and Ashley can become familiar with what I call the "TOP TEN" feelings:

MAD	**EMBARRASSED**
SCARED	**LONELY**
SAD	**BORED**
GLAD	**FRUSTRATED**
JEALOUS	**GUILTY**

As awareness develops, children can increase their vocabulary with more sophisticated synonyms: GLAD can grow to include CONTENTED, JOYFUL, PEACEFUL, PROUD, EXHILARATED, EXCITED, ECSTATIC among others. MAD can be extended to ENRAGED, ANGRY, FURIOUS, IRRITATED, ANNOYED, DISGUSTED. Alex and Ashley can try to recognize which word fits best into a specific situation, gradually acquiring finer discrimination in nuance.

To help your child distinguish the intensity of a feeling, he might be asked to describe 'how happy' or 'how sad' he is feeling on a scale of 1 - 5. With young children colors can be used to make concrete the concept of intensity. MAD is 'red,' SAD is 'blue,' GLAD is 'yellow,' SCARED is 'white.' Even adults describe feelings with color when they say, "I was as white as a sheet." "I was green with envy." "I was so mad I saw red!" Then your child, when experiencing MAD can decide if he feels a 'big red' or maybe just a 'little pink' and together you can determine if his intensity is a reasonable match to the situation. I remember Joey, a learning disabled little fellow, struggling with his spelling. He told me he was so angry at school that day that "it was even more than a 'big red'... it was a 'deep purple'!" He did not yet have the word 'frustrated' in his vocabulary but he had a tool for expressing how he felt.

Remember that your child will 'feel' all those emotions, even the more subtle ones such as guilt, shame or jealousy long before he has the vocabulary to accurately pinpoint what he is feeling. But because he can't express a feeling does not mean he is not struggling with a problem. Unfortunately, when children cannot recognize, understand or express what they feel, they act out instead.

Always try to use a personal reference to discuss the hook-up of some event you have experienced to your own feeling. Encourage your child to share his feelings as well or to recall an event that might match the feeling you have shared. Andy might keep a 'Feelings Log' as a school project, detailing whenever he experiences one of the TOP TEN, or he might interview other people about their emotions, much as a reporter does. Again, literary characters provide a rich source, ever an ongoing lesson, since many times a child might be familiar with a word but yet unable to hook it to a 'feelings awareness.'

I cannot overstress the value of helping your child to acquire a rich 'feelings' vocabulary and to gain 'feelings awareness.' I sincerely believe a child cannot develop into an emotionally healthy adult if he is unable to identify and express what he feels.

FACING FEELINGS

Building a 'feelings' vocabulary serves as a foundation, but facing and then fixing our feelings is another matter. One of my favorite cartoons shows a sagacious old professor bestowing wisdom upon his psychology students as he lectures, "Freud had an interesting thing to say about pain and suffering in life... he said, 'AVOID IT!'"

And that, in a nutshell, tells us why so many people, even those quite articulate, often fail to face their feelings, to acknowledge their existence. Embracing our grief, facing our fear of death, our feeling of abandonment... reliving, through memories, unhappy experiences that had hurt and frightened us may be anticipated as too painful to review, even though common knowledge has taught us that the short term discomfort of remembering proves to carry potential benefits if only one can face, accept, understand and grow beyond the problem.

In addition to avoiding discomfort, it seems that most of us develop the habit of interpreting our feelings, attaching judgments and conclusions about them, often irrationally and superstitiously. Here are a few familiar examples you will recognize:

☹ "I am afraid to feel happy because then something bad is sure to happen."

☹ "If I show that I am afraid, I will be a coward."

☹ "If I show how I feel, everybody will laugh at me."

Sometimes the habit of interpreting and judging ourselves for having a negative feeling leads to what has been called 'giving ourselves a second emotional problem about a first':

☹ "I shouldn't feel afraid... if I am, I will be a coward, and then I'll feel ashamed."

☹ "If I show how I feel everyone will know what a mixed up mess I am. Then I'll still feel depressed and I'll be humiliated too."

☹ "I shouldn't feel happy because that would be selfish. Then I'll feel guilty because I am feeling happy."

What are the implications here for Alex, Ashley or Andy? Can you help your child through this 'avoid and escape' trap? Yes, you can, but it is a developmental process, not a quick fix. In Chapters G and H you will learn how "Growin' Guts" and pursuing "Happiness–A Healthy Sense of Self" are a part of a total picture which encourages your child not to set up impenetrable defenses. Helping children learn to become open and self-disclosing both to themselves and others happens best through modeling by you. Acquiring an adequate vocabulary and an awareness of feelings is necessary but not sufficient. You need to demonstrate that you are willing to run the risk of self-disclosure, and that you will not be critical of your child or discount his feelings when he tries to share them. Trust is involved, you see. Exposing your deepest feelings is basic to building intimate connections, both within yourself and with others.

FIXING FEELINGS

Do you know that many people go through an entire

life without understanding that our emotions are predominantly hooked to our perceptions, to our beliefs, to what we say to ourselves about a situation more than to the actual event? Put simply, WE FEEL AS WE THINK, to a great extent. The late cartoonist, Walt Kelly, said it best. Are you old enough to remember his comic strip character 'Pogo,' that lovable old 'possum of the Okeefenokee Swamp'? One episode portrayed scout Pogo on reconnaissance, reporting to his comrades from high in a tree, "We have met the enemy, —and it is us."

Pogo was right. As it turns out, we cause most of our own upsettedness. Put it another way, "It is difficult to fight an enemy that has outposts in our head." Now don't get me wrong. Life certainly presents us with one hassle after another, to be sure. But only we, with our own negative thinking, manage to escalate stress into feelings of distress. What we do with our heads determines whether we convert disappointments into emotional catastrophes, fear into panic, irritation into rage, or sadness into despair. Emotions are natural and we will always have them... the question is, can we maintain ballast when our ship hits emotional waters? Can we take charge, de-escalating our emotions when they are excessive and hurtful to us, instead of exploding or hiding from them?

I have some GOOD NEWS - BAD NEWS about fixing feelings. The BAD NEWS part is that most of us have been rehearsing illogical thoughts for such a long time that we have developed bad habits of thinking and feeling. One of our hurtful thinking habits is holding onto the common belief that our emotional upsettedness has been caused by other people, especially our parents and that we are victims, permanently crippled by our past experiences. The rest of the BAD NEWS is that altering any kind of habit is difficult, and takes effort. But the GOOD NEWS is that we can change if we really want to, that we do have the power to alter how we feel, no matter our past. And this GOOD NEWS message is the one we want Alex and Ashley to learn.

No matter our past, we do not need to become permanent victims of misfortune or abuse. We are not automatically 'ruined' by our early experiences, as so many people assume. Negative feelings don't wave over us arbitrarily. They derive from memories and thoughts we have long held but which can be examined and reevaluated from a more objective adult perspective.

Adults are not psychologically dependent, while unfortunately, children are. Through the early years Alex, Ashley and Andy are easily impressed by what adults tell them and show them. Because they have limited reasoning skills, they sincerely assume that what adults say is true and unassailable.

Children are natural set-ups for what I call the three 'Fixings'... Formalizing... Fertilizing... and Firmalizing. If, for example, a zealously religious parent tells his child, "Don't do that! You are bad and God will punish you," that idea, immediately followed by emotions of fear and guilt will be 'formalized,' conceptually. If that message is delivered repeatedly, the hook-up of idea and emotion gets 'fertilized' again and again, each time building strength. Eventually the combination becomes a deeply held belief accompanied by a conditioned emotional response. I call that 'firmalized.'

Since children really are dependent upon adults to protect them from harm and to provide a sense of security, the belief that one needs a strong person upon whom to depend or the belief that external events and other people cause us misery is readily 'firmalized.' Long before a child is mature enough to reason independently he has 'firmalized' a whole set of rules... many deeply held beliefs, accompanied by 'firmalized' emotional reactions, which have been poured into his head by adults or have developed from faulty, child-like observations. I like to think of FIXING FEELINGS with young Alex as following that wise old proverb, "an ounce of prevention is worth a pound of cure." As a parent, you can turn that 'fizing' process to a healthy advantage, by gradually 'firmalizing' positive thoughts and feelings with your child as a developmental task. Understanding the 'fizing' process, per se, is not meaningful to children, of course, but the process can be applied successfully, nonetheless, simply by DOING IT, using a variety of activities.

Because children reason poorly, they will have a natural tendency to conclude that bad feelings are caused by 'unlucky or unfair events' or by 'mean, unfair people,' but you can start early to introduce the alternative view that our head talk determines how we feel, not 'mean people.' And the lesson is much better assimilated when your child is not in the midst of an upset! Earlier in this chapter the suggestion was made that you read familiar bedtime stories with your child and investigate the connection between the story action and the feeling experienced by the character. That assignment was fine for teaching 'feelings awareness' but inadequate for teaching the connection between head-talk and feelings. Now I suggest that you amend the assignment. Instead of asking only, "What was Farmer McGregor feeling when Peter Rabbit ate his carrots?" (MAD) follow that with, "What do you think Farmer McGregor said to himself causing him to feel so mad?." ("That terrible rabbit. He shouldn't do that!") When you ask, "How did the little pig feel when the wolf was blowing down the straw house?" (SCARED) ask next, "Yes, but what did the little pig say to himself causing him to feel so afraid?." ("Oh, my goodness! He will eat me up!") At first, you are 'formalizing' the concept that one's head-talk intervenes between an event and a feeling. Repeating over and again the existence of a hook-up between ideas and feelings 'fertilizes' that concept, and eventually, of course, a child internalizes the important awareness that how one thinks and what one says to himself greatly influences his emotions.

The power of this knowledge is profound, and is paramount for a lifetime process of FIXING FEELINGS. This skill enables us to take charge of reprogramming our negative head-talk, to examine current situations in juxtaposition with our habitual responses and thus to understand that we truly have power to overcome influences from our past.

We would be naive to assume that Alex, Ashley and Andy will fully incorporate this knowledge as a child. They won't. When an umpire calls them "OUT" in a baseball game, most likely they will revert to a childish interpretation of "That's not fair!" accompanied by an equally childish demand that the world and everyone in it should be fair, and should never make mistakes. But the seeds are sown.

Working with story characters is merely one activity to help Alex practice hooking his 'thinking' to feelings. Real life experiences are even better teaching devices, once a child has begun to formalize the concept. After Alex has enraged himself by an umpire's decision, he can be calmed and then assisted in confronting his head-talk and in determining whether his internal 'Rules' are reasonable.

Children notoriously show a low frustration tolerance for anger. Years ago some children and I invented the 'turkey game,' designed to give a child practice in controlling his temper under duress. A child would stand in front of a mirror and wait while a few other children would deliberately taunt him by saying, "You are a turkey! Your mother is a turkey!" over and over. The challenge was to see how long the child could stay calm, while he watched for a feather to pop out on his skin. No turkey feathers ever appeared, and we would discuss the 'formalizing' concept that 'just because someone calls you a bad name doesn't mean it is true, so why must you upset yourself about someone else's rude behavior?' If the child held up well under the turkey attack, he told us what he practiced saying to himself to help him stay calm. Repeated practice, of course, leads to firmalizing two healthy Rules: we can stay in charge of our anger and our worth is not defined by other people.

Let me say one more time, we acknowledge that events do contribute to stress. No one wants rain on his parade, no one wants to be called a turkey and nobody likes to be called "OUT!" by an umpire. Let me also remind you from earlier chapters that children are not all alike. Some children are born with biological systems that just naturally are prone to making mountains out of molehills. Those children are especially vulnerable to forming strong conditioned emotional responses from just one negative experience. If they are frightened by a dog, they are likely to become phobic, because they will over-generalize. Reason tells us that not all dogs are vicious, or even that all dogs running and barking are vicious. One frightening dog does not characterize dogs in general, but children do not reason well, and a 'mountain-molehill' child will fall prey to exaggerated emotional responses. They, especially, need continual training lest they circumvent that all-important 'thinking' part of the equation.

Sports psychologists have emphasized the importance of mental imagery in managing emotional distress. They work with athletes teaching them to think positive thoughts and to visualize positive outcomes, procedures that prove the power of self-talk intervention between a potentially stressful event and an emotional outcome. Mental imagery can be very effective with children if they have encountered horror movies followed by nightmares or other fearful responses. My grandson, Andy, a child with a vivid imagination and a mountain-molehill bias, worked out a really ingenious plan with his mother. After Andy has frightened himself with a horror show, he closes his eyes and visualizes the 'monster' coming off a movie set and entering the dressing room. There the 'monster' begins to peel off all his ghoulish costuming and make-up, with Andy visualizing every step of the process, until he 'sees' the monster emerge as a plain actor, who showers, perhaps drinks a coke, dons his street clothes and cheerily waves goodbye to the other actors. By inserting different visual imagery and positive head-talk, Andy has taught himself to handle a potentially stressful event without distress.

A different activity I use with children demonstrates to them how they can make themselves feel upset or calm. They close their eyes and picture an animal, perhaps a cat, entering their room. I direct them to talk 'scary' in their heads and to think of all the terrible things a cat might do to them... bite them, jump on their shoulder, scratch their face, yowl in their ear and to picture the cat doing all those acts. Then I ask them to tell me how they feel (afraid, most will report). Next we wipe the imagery slate clean and start over with another cat. This time they are to tell themselves positive attributes and to picture a cat at their feet, rubbing up to be petted, all floppy and purring, and finally to visualize the cat jumping gently into their lap, curling contentedly in a ball to fall asleep. Now they report if they 'feel any different' (usually calm, no longer afraid, perhaps pleased).

A variation is to provide an image for children that will easily lead to feelings of anger, such as an umpire unfairly causing their team to lose a game, enhanced with plenty of negative head-talk suggested by me, until they can report feeling a 'big red.' Then I ask the children to close their eyes and tone down their anger to feeling merely disappointed and just a little peeved. When they signal success, I ask them to share how they did it. Invariably, they describe a change in their head-talk. From these activities comes a concrete experience and discussion about how our feelings are very much affected by what we say to ourselves, what we anticipate and what expectations we hold.

The realization that thoughts, more than events, control our feelings may be unfamiliar to you and thus not yet a working concept for you to teach your child. If so, let me share with you the more scientific approach to the lesson that I take with young adult college students. To demonstrate to the class, I name four students to form a small group with pencil and paper. My selection of students is random, but they do not know this. I announce that I will whisper a message in their ear and they are to write one predominant feeling they experience as a result.

Unknown to them, every student receives the same negative message, "I do not think you are qualified to be a graduate student and I have misgivings about you, both intellectually and in your class attitude." (This task is most onerous for me, but I persevere because it serves as an excellent teaching device.) The students each write their feeling word and then I explain to the class the purpose of the demonstration, hopefully to prove that our thinking determines how we feel. Each student shares aloud his feeling recorded. Consistently the students will produce a variety of emotions to an identical stimulus event. Thus the event, alone, could not possibly have caused the response, according to the scientific law of cause and effect. The experiment demonstrates graphically that an intervening thought process plays a significant role in how one feels. Detective work follows as the class identifies each student's unique head-talk. Typically, if a student felt FEAR... the head-talk was, "Dr. Campbell controls my grade. I must get an A or B to bring up my grade point average... I'm in real trouble," resulting in FEAR. If another student thought, "Dr. Campbell has no right to judge me like that. She barely knows me yet. How dare she conclude that I am not smart!," this head-talk resulted in ANGER. A third student might often have concluded, "I knew it. Dr. Campbell has discovered how stupid I really am. I'll never be able to get a decent grade."... this head-talk having led to HOPELESSNESS, DESPAIR.

All three emotional responses were predictable, once the individual head-talk was exposed. As a bit of levity, however, I must confess that one time a student really caught me short when she reported her feeling as PITY. I had to admit to the class that I was stuck and could not predict her intervening interpretation. Said she, "I thought, poor Dr. Campbell... if she evaluated me so completely wrong, she must be a terrible psychologist... how sad for her!"

FIXING FEELINGS goes beyond the detective work of identifying your head-talk and finding those deeply held 'Firmalized Rules' which trigger your negative emotions. Find them, but then hold them up for scrutiny. Do they really make sense? Is it really true that if a dog scares you that means all dogs are frightening? Is it really true that if your mother doesn't love you that means you are not lovable? Is it for sure that if you make a mistake, your goof 'proves' you are a fool and incompetent? If today feels 'awful,' does it follow that tomorrow and thereafter will never get better?

Cognitive psychologists label that particular type of inquiry as the 'Where is the proof? Question'... an excellent confrontation to help you determine whether your head-talk and your 'Rules' are rational or irrational.

You might not only ask yourself "Will an 'Awful Today' really guarantee an 'Awful Forever'?" but might follow it with a second question, "Is my evaluation of 'Awful' accurate or an exaggeration? Is my discomfort 'So Awful' that I really can't stand it?" The answer, of course, is that you can stand it, because you are standing it and if you truly couldn't, you would be psychotic or dead, which you are not. Most times, when people excessively upset themselves by 'Awfulizing' they could learn to de-escalate their level of discomfort from panic, rage or 'deep purple' frustration down to a more manageable feeling of merely displeased or disappointed. Cognitive psychologists refer to that second type of inquiry as the 'Awfulizing Question.' Finally, you can confront yourself with two other good questions: first, "Do I have the power to alter this stressful condition, this event, or this person who seems to be hassling me?" If so, make your plans and take an action! If not, ask a second question of yourself, "How will I feel if I cannot change the event and yet I refuse to change how I am thinking?" The answer to that, of course, is that you will continue to feel miserable, hardly a goal worth pursuing.

Can children handle these sophisticated inquiries? No, not very well at first, not successfully when they are young and not without help. But it is never too early to sow the seeds for rational living and emotional well-being. Gradually, as a developmental program, your child can learn about his feelings: to be aware of them, to label them, to face and accept them, and to share them. He can begin to appreciate and 'firmalize' the important truth that what he says to himself greatly affects how he feels; that while the events in his world may cause him hassle, he is not a victim nor powerless to manage his feelings and his behavior. He can learn, through doing activities to use visual imagery and positive head-talk in de-escalating inevitable upsets, bringing him a sense of ballast and self-confidence.

Today, if grandson Andy were to ask again, "Grandma, what are feelings?" I think I would be ready. I would tell him:

> *"Feelings come from inside you. They wave over you and when they do, you get happy or sad or mad or scared. When you were a baby, you seemed to have only two feelings, 'happy' or 'upset.' When you were happy, you were peaceful and you smiled and laughed and played and learned about things. When you were upset and not happy*

you cried and screamed and whined and could not do much else. In fact, how you were feeling really affected what you did.

"Feelings wave over you very soon after something happens that is important to you and right after your brain thinks about it. After a while, feelings fade away unless you keep on remembering and thinking about what happened over and over again, like rerunning a TV tape and you make it stay important to you. Then you get the same feeling again, even though what happened to you before isn't really happening anymore. Sometimes, if a feeling hurts a lot, you might hide from that feeling and pretend you don't have it, sort of like stuffing a bad report card in your closet and hoping it will never come out. But that doesn't really work too well, because sooner or later there will be trouble.

"Feelings are very important. Think of your feelings as the steering wheel on your car, and you are the driver. Your brain is the boss of the steering wheel, but the steering wheel is what makes the car go exactly where it goes. If you don't think while you are driving, your steering wheel will bring you plenty of trouble. The same with you. Your thinking brain is the boss of your feelings, but where you end up going, what you say and what you do depends a lot on your feelings. Lucky for us, how we think can keep our 'feeling wheel' from running

us off our road. How we think affects how we feel."

NORMA'S NUGGET:

**FEELING UPSET?
FIND YOUR HEAD-TALK AND
YOUR 'FIRMALIZED RULE.'
CHECK THEM OUT AND
CHANGE YOUR THINKING.
THEN PRACTICE THE
CHANGING ROUTINE
AT LEAST 10 TIMES.**

GROWIN' GUTS, WITH GRIT

... "You can't be brave if you've only had wonderful things happen to you!"
... Mary Tyler Moore

I remember well our family breakfast, almost fifty years ago, because we had the same exchange every morning. Our mother would hand my brother his orange juice and he would say, "I don't want it, orange juice has strings and makes me gag," whereupon Mom would retort, "So what? You don't need to enjoy your orange juice, you drink it to make your insides healthy." Next I would start with "Idonwanna drink my milk. I hate the way it tastes." And Mom would repeat, "So what? Drink it anyway because it makes your teeth and bones strong." Then at dinnertime, the same message... "Hate you spinach? SO WHAT? How many times must I tell you that liking doesn't matter. You eat spinach to make your blood strong."

'SO WHAT' wasn't restricted solely to our eating habits, either, much to my disappointment. After dinner my sister and I cleaned the kitchen together. She preferred to wash the dishes, and I to dry, a perfect combo. Every night we sailed through this routine, often singing duets while we worked. Should have been a parent's dream, right? Wrong. About once a week Mom would come into the kitchen and chastise my sister, "Why are you always washing and letting Norma dry?" My sister, several years older than I, would defend, "because we both like it better this way... Norma hates to wash, and drying the dishes bores me. Can't you just let us be?" And Mom would reply, "No, because doing only pleasant tasks isn't good for you. Every day you should do something you don't like to do. You have to practice being strong!"

And so went our family life. We three children persisted valiantly trying to sidestep our IDONWANNA'S, while our mother doggedly persisted making sure we did not! From that determined lady we gradually internalized some important messages about life. Obvious, of course, was learning that what we eat matters in building a healthy body, but far more relevant was my introduction to that unpalatable truism that what turns out to be 'good for you' often involves doing hard or uncomfortable tasks. Alas... what a revolting discovery for free-spirited children who would much prefer to chase GIMMEEs and LEMMEEs, unimpeded!

Only as a psychologist twenty years later did I come to appreciate the therapeutic value of those two words my mother invoked so frequently, "SO WHAT?." I observed many people suffering from inadequate self-confidence and low self-esteem with a connection between their unhappiness and low frustration tolerance for discomfort. Distressed people certainly will tend to display low frustration tolerance (we call this LFT in the psych biz), but I found the cause-effect relationship can be the reverse... attempts to continually avoid discomfort, at all costs, often result in unhappiness. Many people with LFT lack emotional strength. They feel weak and fearful. Just those two words, "SO WHAT," when proffered, not with derision but with empathy and as rational inquiry, can provide a foundation powerful enough to overcome fears and other incapacitating thoughts and feelings. I firmly believe that parents can help children not only with their physical well being, but their emotional growth through deliberate choices. 'Growin' up good' must incorporate what I call GROWIN' GUTS, WITH GRIT and that's what this chapter is about.

Think of the hours a child is required to practice reading or to master his spelling words, No sensible parent assumes those skills will be acquired incidentally and we expect educators to define and measure our child's progress. Encouraging your child to take risks, to go forth bravely for the purpose of developing confidence is not so easily defined, however, and schools are not able to measure or guarantee success in a course called 'bravery.'

GROWIN' GUTS can be programmed. The training program includes teaching your child to incorporate some tough head talk like, "SO WHAT? I CAN STAND THAT!" and then to practice acting upon a difficult decision. When I counsel upset people, they quickly hear from me that gaining insight is only half of the therapy process... the easy half. The other half is leaving my office with an assignment to practice new ways of thinking, of talking to oneself, and then deliberately acting differently, even though to do so feels uncomfortable, initially. If they comply, feelings of genuine pride and self-confidence are immediately experienced, and a grain of courage has been sown.

Notice the word PRIDE. The concept of pride can play havoc with the pursuit of emotional health, I have discovered. Many adults and probably all children do not understand the difference between what I label false pride vs true pride. The underpinnings of false pride is a neurotic and usually fruitless search for security and acceptance through admiration from others. But how worrisome to be continually victimized by the vagaries of whether or not other people are impressed with you! True pride, on the other hand, cannot be gifted from one person to another. You cannot bestow it upon your child, like a birthday present, much as you might desire. What you can do for your child is 'prime the courage pump,' sending the message "I have confidence that you can handle tough problems and come out OK." You can provide opportunities for him to behave bravely and gently nudge him into persisting under adversity.

I have a program for helping your child to GROW GUTS. It is extremely simple and does not involve much explaining, just ongoing activity. With it, children are not required to grasp abstract principles, so you can start them fairly young. The learning is in the doing, and I promise you it will work. Your child will increase his internal strength every time he faces discomfort and chooses to persevere.

TOUGH TILLY AND TOUGH TONY

I have used the activities described here with children of all ages for many years. The program can be effective for just a single child in your family, or as a group effort. Your vocabulary and choice of stories might need to be adjusted for age differences, but the message remains the same. The younger you start, the better. By the time your child is of kindergarten age, start a dialogue like this:

Q: "What do we have to do to build strong bones?"
A: "Drink milk and exercise."

Q: "How do we get strong muscles in our arms and legs?"
A: "Eat meat/fish and exercise."

Q: "Can anyone give you strong muscles as a birthday present?"
A: "No."

Q: "Why not?"
A: "Because that is silly. You must do it for yourself."

Q: "How do we build strong guts to make us brave?"
A: (Usually a child cannot answer.)

"This is a different kind of strong and it doesn't come from eating, but it is a special exercise. You practice doing hard and scary things and you get brave and strong. The more you practice, the braver you get, just as you get stronger muscles when you exercise. Every time you act bravely, you feel strong and powerful inside, and that is like growing guts. BRAVE really means that you felt afraid or it was hard to do, but you did it anyway."

Draw a picture of TOUGH TONY or TOUGH TILLY that looks like this:

Tough Tony **Tough Tilly**

Explain to your child:

"Every time you act bravely or do something really hard, which is just like growing a bit of strong guts, you can color one box. First you do something tough or scary, and then tell me about it. If we agree, you can color in the box. When they are all filled you can earn a good-soldier award and then we'll hang up another picture and start again."

Under Tony or Tilly list the following actions that qualify as 'gut-builders' and for young children you might need to add pictures to go with the words:

GUT BUILDERS
EVERYDAY, DO SOMETHING: • BRAVE, SCARY ... (don't run away!) • BORING ... (don't quit or complain!) • TIRING ... (don't quit or complain!) • MAYBE EMBARRASSING AND EVERYBODY MIGHT LAUGH ... (so what?) • VERY HARD TO LEARN ... (keep trying!) • KIND AND HELPFUL ... (don't tell anyone or ask for thanks) • RESPONSIBLE TO YOURSELF ... (keep your promise!) • OVER-THE-TOP: LEARNING A NEW SKILL ... (hooray!)

Please remember that this activity must be repeated over and over again, much as you would repeat a nursery rhyme or sing the alphabet song endlessly with your little one. The learning occurs gradually. When your child grows beyond the primary grades, a picture of TOUGH TILLY or TOUGH TONY may seem foolish, and you can change to a more sophisticated list:

GUT BUILDERS

TRY SOMETHING . . .

- even though you might look foolish.
- even though you might be wrong and make a goof.
- even though you might fail totally.
- even though you are afraid it might hurt.

. . . . . SO WHAT?

DON'T QUIT . . .

- even though you feel frustrated.
- even though you feel tired and uncomfortable.
- even though you feel discouraged.
- even though you feel bored.
- even though you feel angry.

. . . . . SO WHAT?

DON'T RUN AWAY . . .

- even though you feel afraid!

. . . . . SO WHAT?

SAY TO YOURSELF, "NO! NOT NOW" . . .

- even though you want a GIMMEE really badly.
- when somebody tries to make you do something bad and calls you a chicken.

. . . . . SO WHAT?

BE A GOOD SPORT WITHOUT COMPLAINING . . .

- even though it isn't fair.
- even though you lose.
- even though you can't have it your way.
- even though someone teases you when you look silly.
- even though you aren't the most important person.

. . . . . SO WHAT?

YIELD GRACEFULLY – "UNCLE!" . . .

- by apologizing when you hurt someone.
- by admitting when you are wrong.
- by compromising when you can't agree.
- by not fussing or getting 'even'.
- by complimenting someone who beats you in a game.

STAND UP AND TELL ALOUD . . .

- about making a goof or being wrong.
- a joke about yourself, and laugh at yourself.

Encourage your Alex and Ashley to be specific in identifying events likely to challenge them. The more concrete, the better. Here is a list of situations typically encountered by children once they start school, any of which could be viewed as opportunities for GROWING GUTS. It is legitimate and healthy to allow your child to acknowledge that the situation is uncomfortable and not of his choosing before expecting him to begin gut-building.

The list, of course, is endless. The important message is that children need some structured focus for developing frustration tolerance, too precious a commodity to leave for incidental happenstance.

THINGS I HATE... BUT I CAN STAND!

- my brother/sister bothering me
- kids laughing at me
- pain, when I feel sick, fall down, get a shot
- losing a game
- making a mistake in my work
- having to copy my paper over again
- someone teasing me or calling me names
- mean, unfair teachers
- somebody ordering me around, telling me what to do
- somebody mad at me
- somebody not being fair
- waiting for my turn when I am bored or tired
- doing a pesky job I really dislike
- finishing my paper and having to check my answers
- feeling scared or sad or embarrassed
- getting blamed for something I didn't do
- saying to myself, "NO! NOT NOW," when I really want something
- chilling out when I want to explode

YIELDING

I think the topic of YIELDING requires special attention. Everybody has a boss, sometimes, yet learning to yield gracefully, when it is appropriate, is one of the most difficult 'gut-building' activities for children to accept. Adults, too! One of the ironies of life is the disgusting discovery that while nobody wants to be bossed... everybody has a boss. No one escapes. There is always some person or force stronger or more powerful than you, in some way. Mother nature is probably the most powerful of all... she can tip over a boat, blow down houses and burn forests. At a more personal level, she can drown us, choke us, burn or dismember us in an instant. While that awareness certainly can be discomforting, it is not humiliating. It doesn't demean our worth.

When I was a kid, we played a game called 'King of the Hill,' and the idea was to prove you were more powerful than anyone else, by throwing all the other kids off the hill. The theme was always the same..being the boss! And the supreme game of power was making another kid shout 'UNCLE!' thereby acknowledging defeat of weakness to power. Funny thing for me about that 'UNCLE.' As a child I realized that my motive was not pleasure in dominating another kid, but seeking guaranteed relief that I would not have to shout 'UNCLE!' To me, yielding felt exquisitely painful, eliciting feeling of humiliation and helplessness. UGH! To be avoided at all cost! I used to wonder whether this 'yielding agony' was peculiar solely to me, reflecting my personal vulnerability. Forty years later I have concluded I certainly was not unique. Quite the opposite... I believe one of the most underestimated troubles in emotional upsettedness is what I call the 'stubborn-stupid' factor, encountered too frequently in relationship problems. One or both partners are blocked by the irrational belief that to yield equates to humiliation and worthlessness, no matter what the confrontational issue. Wars are fought over perceived insults and attempts to control. Negotiations and compromises get stalled over the problem of 'yielding' and 'saving face.' This occurs between nations, between mates, between parent and child, and certainly among children. If ever a generalization seems to hold true in emotional upsettedness, it might be that "yielding feels terrible!" Experts ponder whether this power pursuit is more natural in men than women. Perhaps, but I see that neither sex owns 'stubborn-stupid'... it comes in all sizes, shapes and ages, and it can start young.

Often children naively wish they could be grown up so, "Nobody will tell me what to do or boss me around any more." You can commiserate with your child that no one likes to be bossed or forced to yield against our will, especially when we don't like the outcome. We all would rather win than lose a game... we would rather be right than wrong in an argument and no one wants to call 'UNCLE,' but in the real world it happens to all of us, and not just children. EVERYBODY HAS TO YIELD SOMETIMES... we can't always be the biggest and strongest or the smartest, and no one is always right. Sometimes other people will have more power than you and sometimes they will have better ideas, too. Giving in does not mean you are weak or dumb. Accepting conditions and following rules really does not diminish your worth. But if you act 'stubborn-stupidly' when it doesn't make sense, problems only get worse. It's no big deal to call "UNCLE" and you do not need to feel foolish. In fact, just the opposite, you can feel proud and strong because you acted like a good sport and acted wisely even though it was hard to do. Yielding at the right time, in a good-sport manner, builds guts.

Help your child practice and FIRMALIZE this head-talk:

- Everybody has a boss... that's life.
- I can stand rules and having someone tell me what to do.
- Stronger people might be able to make me say 'UNCLE' but that doesn't mean I'm a wimp or that they are right.
- It doesn't feel good to lose, but it isn't AWFUL and doesn't mean I am an inferior person.
- I can admit I was wrong about that. Being wrong doesn't mean I am stupid, and nobody can be right every time.
- Giving in is no fun, but I can do it, and build guts.
- If I yield, I may feel embarrassed a little, but I don't have to feel humiliated or shamed.

Model for your child. Tell about your own foibles, and admit to feeling a little foolish, but not devastated. Let him hear you apologize and admit when you have behaved stubbornly. Read with him stories about characters who understand how to yield graciously. Children need to hear over and again some variation of 'to lose a game... does not mean shame' and 'a good sport thinks... cheating stinks!' Keep at the project until your child can handle this humorous rhyme:

> 'UNCLE! UNCLE!' I can play it.
> (Even though I hate to say it!)
> If today I'm not the boss,
> Giving in is no big loss.
> I don't need to wail or burn
> Maybe next will be my turn.
> And even if it's not... So what?

Wish I could tell you this 'yielding' project were easy, but it is not, and takes much practice. Unfortunately, a long established habit of stubbornly refusing to yield seems to become functionally autonomous, developing a life of its own, extremely difficult to alter. That is why it is important for you to start early helping your child to discriminate between yielding according to the logic of the situation and not according to some feeling of anticipatory humiliation.

POPSICLES AND NOODLES

By now you can see that 'growin' guts' takes effort and is not easy. So, I really try to use graphic phrases that suggest visual imagery to help people remain resolute when they feel upset. One may not be able to avoid stressful situations but the goal is learning to handle inevitable stress without undue distress. Despite the humorous absurdity of these images, they have proved to be most effective tools for adults, not just children. Try them yourself and then invoke them with your Alex and Ashley.

When a person feels bad and comes to seek help, I will

empathize long enough for him to know that I am attending and caring. But, eventually I will say something like:

> *"You must ask yourself two important questions that will affect our plan of action. First, ask yourself, 'AM I A POPSICLE?' and then, 'AM I A NOODLE?'"*

Let me explain about popsicles. Popsicles cannot survive in an unfriendly environment. As soon as the popsicle leaves the freezer it is vulnerable to total obliteration. If dropped, it cracks. If exposed to heat, it melts. If rained upon, it washes away. We might say that the survival of a popsicle is precarious, at best. This is an issue to face as we contemplate your dilemma. Just exactly how weak are you, internally? Will you crack, melt, or disappear into nothingness when you hit a life hassle? Or, more realistically, will you feel uncomfortable? You may, in fact, have a nervous system that just naturally makes big deals out of little deals, and if so, handling stress for you may be a big challenge... but even so, couldn't you stand that? Would you actually be destroyed, or really just discomforted?

How about, 'AM I A NOODLE?' Noodles are weak and floppy. They get tangled and twisted, quite at the mercy of the spaghetti twirler in command. If you are a noodle person you will likely feel helpless

> *and frustrated, not knowing that probably you can do much more for yourself than you believe. You may procrastinate and agonize, remaining in perpetual misery because you do not remind yourself that taking an action usually beats sitting on your duff feeling like a victim."*

Many a former client has told me years later that they have continued to evoke the images of POPSICLES and NOODLES whenever confronted with a critical life hassle. Those two colorful labels endure as cues in their memory. Children, even more than adults, of course, best absorb concepts which are presented concretely and involve action. They grasp POPSICLES and NOODLES. Explaining them to children requires very few words. The covert message is that you may not like discomfort but you can stand it when it is appropriate and in your best interests to endure frustration, irritation, or even unavoidable pain. This is not intended as a lesson in denial... the suggestion is not to pretend that you do not have feelings, but rather is an exercise in short-term frustration tolerance and long term emotional maturity, one of the goals for helping Alex and Ashley in 'growin' up good.'

NORMA'S NUGGET:

'I AM NOT A POPSICLE' IS A CONCRETE REMINDER THAT I CAN STAND DISCOMFORT, WHILE 'I AM NOT A NOODLE' REMINDS ME THAT I CAN TAKE DIFFICULT ACTIONS . . . I DO NOT NEED TO BE A VICTIM.

Chapter 

HAPPINESS IS... A HEALTHY SENSE OF SELF, WITH HUMOR!

... The greater part of our happiness or misery depends on our disposition and not on our circumstances.
... Martha Washington

One of the all-time favorite jokes circulating among teachers some years ago went like this: A primary teacher noticed that one of her pupils habitually came to school unkempt and odiferous. Concerned that the child might be socially rejected, she sent home a pleasant but direct note suggesting that the parents bathe their child. The next day the little fellow arrived at school still unkempt, with an equally polite note from his mother: "Dear teacher, please don't smell Johnny, learn him."

One humorous mother not withstanding, parents are almost unanimous in requesting professionals to PLEASE HELP MY CHILD FEEL HAPPY AND GOOD ABOUT HIMSELF. That sounds like a reasonable enough request. Psychologists may posit many diverse philosophies about human behavior and how best to help children 'grow up good,' but they are probably unanimous in the belief that the cornerstone of enduring happiness is good mental health and the internalizing of a positive sense of self. Now, hypothesizing that bathing an odiferous child would benefit him socially is hardly controversial. Far less unanimous, however, is agreement among the experts about how you define and promote such an elusive concept as feeling good about oneself. Popular buzz words abound such as 'Self-Esteem,' 'Self-Concept' and 'Self-Image' but I discovered that experts have had a heck of a time trying to either define those terms or measure how a child feels about himself! After 10,000 scientific studies on self-esteem, for example, researchers still are unable to agree on what 'self-esteem' is. Even 100 teachers, when asked to define 'self-esteem' came up with 27 distinctively different answers. No wonder trying to promote a positive self-concept in a child looms a nebulous task. So just what is a positive sense of self, and what is this elusive thing called HAPPINESS? And how can we get it for our children?

Several authorities emphasize encouraging and praising a child for any or all of his efforts, no matter how good or awful the product, as the way to build self-concept. Others disagree, insisting that adults should never let a child settle for less than he is capable of giving. Still others insist that adults pass no judgment whatsoever, not even praise, and they eschew awarding any form of prizes or grades, lest rating a child's skill destroy his creative juices, or train him to rely upon external stroking as a measure of his worth.

Some authorities insist that an abundance of toys and positive regard will not spoil a child; only failing to set limits on acceptable behavior will. But, we might ask, does a 'spoiled child' have high self-esteem? And, can one receive too much esteem? Yes, some experts believe a child can, in fact, receive so much indulgent 'good will' from his parents that he actually becomes too precious...

holding himself in such high esteem that he dominates everybody else. You have already learned about just such entitlement in previous chapters. A very famous boxer may have epitomized this 'too precious' syndrome when he once remarked, "When you're as great as I am, it is hard to be humble." So here we have this dilemma about a positive sense of self. Professionals can't seem to define it precisely, we don't have agreement on how to promote it, but somehow we think we recognize it when we see it and we seem to agree that it is foundational for enduring contentment.

I have a problem with the term 'self-esteem' not only because the concept of esteem can misguide a child into rating himself as a superior being, but because it reinforces an absolutistic superior-inferior dichotomy of worth. Unfortunately, children seem naturally prone to evaluate their core being in black-white categories of 'wonderful' vs 'worthless,' a rating system too easily extended to judging others. To me, 'growin' up good' means attending to both the serenity within your child and harmony between himself and others, so I propose an entirely different definition and approach.

Alex and Ashley's positive sense of self might be conceptualized as developing along four component tracks: SELF-CONFIDENCE, SELF-RESPECT, SELF-ACCEPTANCE and SELF-AWARENESS. I believe each component contributes to your child's understanding and appreciation not only of himself, but others.

SELF-CONFIDENCE derives from a positive belief and self-statement, "I can tackle and master difficult skills, I am not helpless."

SELF-RESPECT results directly from a positive

experience in which one has acted bravely and persistently and internalizes this self-statement, "I am feeling proud of how I acted because I hung tough, no matter win-or-lose, even when I didn't feel comfortable, or didn't feel appreciated." Both self-confidence and self-respect are the fabric of that true pride described in the previous chapter GROWIN' GUTS, WITH GRIT.

SELF-ACCEPTANCE is quite different and apart from true pride. Positive self-acceptance derives, paradoxically, not from the belief "I am wonderful and superior" but rather from an internal dialogue, "I totally and completely accept myself as a person whose behaviors are often foolish and laughable, yet who is always worthy, always lovable, simply by virtue of being human. I am neither good nor bad. I am not wonderful nor terrible. I simply am... human." A subtle but crucial distinction exists between rating one's personage as opposed to objectively observing and rating one's behavior, all the while unconditionally accepting oneself, under every circumstance. Please do not misunderstand this message delivered to your child. How one behaves most certainly matters! Through our religious teachings, codes of moral ethics and civilized standards of justice and equality we have no dearth of mandates defining which behaviors are acceptable and which are not. The developmental task here is helping Alex, Ashley and Andy to understand and accept the abstract (but oh, so terribly important) concept that our core of worth, because of our humanness, always remains the same, even though we may totally disapprove of our behavior. In fact, an irony exists in that unless one can separate rating his worth from rating his behavior, he is unlikely to succeed at altering unacceptable habits. This distinction proves so difficult to internalize that I often present, not only to children, but even to sophisticated adults suffering from a 'bad me' depression, a concrete picture of two child-like cookie figures, side by side. One figure (A) is labeled I AM WHAT I DO and the other (B) I AM HUMAN.

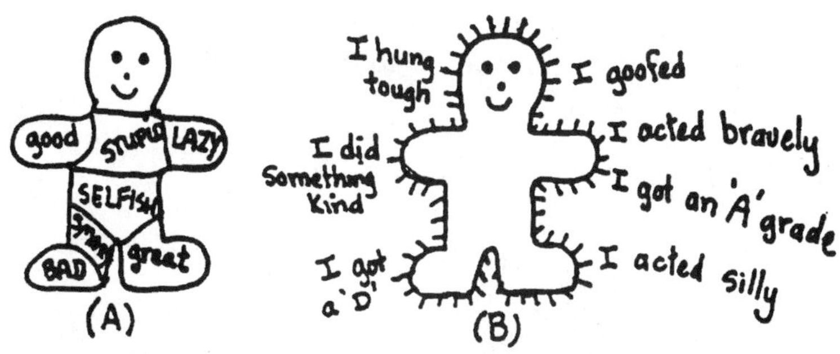

**I AM WHAT I DO.
WHAT I DO DEFINES
MY WORTH. I RATE
AND RANK MYSELF.**

**I AM HUMAN.
WHAT I DO MATTERS
BUT DOES NOT
DEFINE MY WORTH.
I RATE AND RANK
MY BEHAVIORS,
BUT NOT ME.**

I AM WHAT I DO goes with this head talk:

- ☹ I am good or I am bad.
  This is the way I am.
- ☹ If I do everything right I am a good person.
- ☹ If I make mistakes I am a bad person.

- ☹ I don't want to know about my bad behaviors or else I will feel badly about myself and I will be a bad person.
- ☹ I must do wonderful things so everybody will think I am great and I can agree and have high self-esteem.
- ☹ I always make mistakes so I think I am hopeless. I am stuck with my badness.

I AM HUMAN goes with this head talk:

- ☺ I am human, so I will goof sometimes.
- ☺ I can laugh at me and still feel OK because I am neither good nor bad . . . I am human.
- ☺ I do many things every day . . .
  some are good, some are bad, some are nice, some are smart, some are not! My behaviors don't live inside of me and they don't measure my worth.
- ☺ I can look at my behaviors and decide if I want to change some, and still choose to feel good about me. If I get a "C" grade, that doesn't mean I am a "C" person.

With these models Alex and Ashley can be helped to understand that if they choose to believe the model of cookie-person (A) they are often likely to feel sad, anxious or frustrated because they will always worry about having to do everything perfectly. Now this just isn't possible, since everyone does hundreds of things every day, some of which will be desirable and some not. So, under this model (A), a child will not want to admit to a mistake. He will degrade his worth every time he performs imperfectly or competitively measures his score against others, with his worth on the line according to the outcome. He will tend to feel hopeless and to believe he is 'stuck' permanently with his 'badness,' telling himself, "This is the way I am." Cookie person (A) will conclude that if he gets a 'C' grade that proves he is no better than a 'C' person.

Another problem with cookie person (A) is that even if someone could manage to perform perfectly, thus 'proving' his superior personage, the concept of 'superior' connotes 'more special than someone else,' not a good way to think about other people and which does not lead to harmonious living. If children learn to accept and believe the model of cookie person (B) they can always remain peaceful about themselves, no matter what they achieve or do not achieve, since their worth is not measured by what they do. In this model, their worth is not even really contingent upon 'doing the best you can' because, although it is admirable to try, no one can or will do his best at all times. That is simply not the human way. The most superior athletes, for example, do not perform well on every occasion. Yet people can learn to accept themselves, even with their worst errors, and this acceptance, paradoxically, often leads to better behaviors. Most people who continuously misbehave prove to hold poor self-images, mired in feelings of guilt, despair and hopelessness. Under model (B) if your child can totally accept himself as human under ALL conditions without self-condemnation, he will be free to examine his behaviors more objectively, a generosity he can also extend to others. Rating and ranking behaviors, both of oneself and others, without the ideation of superior-inferior categories is totally appropriate and is one cornerstone to harmonious living. Learning to unconditionally accept oneself, and then others, starts at as simple a level as helping your child to recognize and state aloud, "If I get a 'C' grade, that does not make me a 'C' person!"

In summary, Alex and Ashley are learning: WHAT YOU DO MATTERS, BUT, YOU ARE NOT WHAT YOU DO. Model (B) has an equally important corollary, however, which is: EVERYBODY GOOFS, A LOT... TRY TO ACCEPT THIS ABOUT YOURSELF AND LEARN TO LAUGH AT YOUR MISTAKES. Caring parents and teachers work hard to teach their children to believe, "I am lovable and capable," but tend not to emphasize self-humor as well. Learning to laugh at oneself takes practice! It almost seems as if humans have a built-in, ready-made humiliation button, triggered by the slightest provocation. Alex and Ashley can learn that since everyone goofs a lot, everyone is laughable. So they can be taught to believe, "I am lovable and capable... AND laughable."

If a child can accept that making goofs does not mean "I am a goof-person" he can understand, "I don't need to feel so badly every time I make a mistake. Many goofs are really funny, and make other people laugh. Since everyone will be laughing at my behavior but not my worth, I can laugh too. Maybe I will feel a little silly when I discover I made a goof, but I do not need to feel humiliated or ashamed unless I forget and think like cookie-model (A)."

There is a secret about laughing, too. Laughing chases away bad feelings. Humans are both lovable and laughable and these qualities are not mutually exclusive. They don't conflict, they complement each other. The most beloved comedians proved to be masters at humorously poking fun at their own foibles, Jack Benny and Bill Cosby to name a few. They are endearingly lovable to us, even when we don't know them personally. We love them for their fallible 'humanness.' Today the entire world reveres the memory of Lucille Ball who epitomized the combination of lovable and laughable in her "I Love Lucy" role.

Everybody goofs. That is just plain true. We make errors in judgement, errors in prediction and errors in execution and we seem to make them again and again. If we don't make those, we commit errors of omission, by failing to act at all. Face it, humans goof. Parents can serve as models in a helpful family project I call 'Goof-and-Tell.' At dinnertime you can share one of your own goofs and encourage the entire family to laugh and enjoy the humor, poking fun at you. By modeling self-humor your child will be encouraged to take his turn admitting and describing aloud a foolish goof. Sometimes, of course, a mistake is not funny, and it would be more appropriate to feel sad, if someone had been hurt or offended in some way. If so, help your child to think through and verbalize, "If my mistake hurt someone, I can apologize and pay back in some way, to show that I am sorry and willing to be responsible. I can hate what I did, but still accept myself, and try not to make that mistake again." If you wish, you can allow your Alex or Ashley to fill in one Tough Tony (Tilly) bar for being brave enough to share a goof with good humor and for allowing others to laugh. You might sing this jingle with young children to help them accept themselves as imperfect "GOOFERS" which goes to the tune of "100 Bottles of Beer on the Wall":

99 foolish goofs in my life,
99 foolish goofs . . .
I used one up, I laughed at myself . . .
98 goofings left in my life . . . etc

If your child is older than primary age he might appreciate and benefit from this rhyme:

ON GOOFING

Oh, how foolish I can be!
Goodness, what is wrong with me?
Absolutely nothing... hey!
People goof up every day.
None of us can hold up long
Making not one goof or wrong.
You need never hide in shame
'Cause your worth remains the same.
Self-condemning needs a rest!
Try to settle for your best.
Laugh, and get this through you head...
You will goof 'til you are dead!

SELF-AWARENESS, the last component in building a positive sense of self, includes a belief and self-statement, "I am a person, uniquely me. I am valuable because I am human. I have ideas, beliefs, opinions and feelings which are my habits. I have many strengths, but weaknesses, too. Put all my parts together and I am one-of-a-kind, a unique person called ME. I need to know me well since I will be living entirely with myself all my life. And I have a good brain too, so I had better let my computer brain be 'user friendly' to me. Alex and Ashley need to internalize the message I WILL LIVE CONSTANTLY WITH MYSELF ALL OF MY LIFE so they will gradually realize that happiness and contentment ultimately derives from within, and will appreciate the importance of self-awareness.

Self-awareness is part of a personal plan and mapping a personal plan is quite like developing any mapping skill... it is very hard to figure out how to get somewhere if you don't know where you are now. For young children, awareness often begins with school units including popular activities such as describing one's family, denoting favorite activities, tastes and interests. While these are useful as a start, they are not sufficient for helping a child to really discover himself, to acknowledge his feelings, beliefs and habits. However, being open to oneself can occur only if a person has self-acceptance, confidence and courage. That is why this self-awareness component can develop only in conjunction with the others.

Did you notice that each component emphasized encouraging Alex and Ashley to hold positive self-statements? Do not assume that your child knows how to think and talk positively. Many people seem to be just naturals for 'stinking thinking' and you might need to interrupt your child's negative self-assessing habits. Do not let him put himself down. Several years ago while doing research at a university campus school some colleagues and I discovered that children labeled as 'low self-esteem' pupils (identified both by their teachers and a measuring scale) had no repertoire of verbal, positive images about themselves. Specifically, when asked, or even rewarded, they could not verbalize one positive self-statement. This was distinctly different from children rated by teachers as holding good 'self-esteem' from whom a variety of positive self-statements emanated with ease. We modeled, prompted and encouraged the low self-esteem children to rehearse positive self-statements over and over, helping them to establish a repertoire, and guess what? Their 'self-esteem' as measured on that self-concept scale caught up to the other children. Positive head-talk really works. We know, for example, that non-assertive persons can acquire genuine feelings of new inner strength and confidence AFTER practicing to say and do assertive behaviors even when they did not feel confident in advance. People really learn by doing and attitude changes can follow as readily as precede action.

CONCLUSION: LIFE'S RATIONAL RULES

During your child's formative years, both caring parents and teachers put much effort into helping Alex and Ashley acquire academic skills, meticulously defining and monitoring their progress in the famous Three R's. Too bad the development of a fourth R has not yet been given equal emphasis. Despite the common knowledge that character, attitude, work habits and motivation are just as crucial as academic skills in promoting life-long satisfaction, we have not yet committed to specifically program and track a child's social and emotional maturity. I have come to define this fourth R: 'Rational Rules of the World.'

Many years ago I was struggling to help one young

woman to grow up emotionally. We were not succeeding very well, and I was incredulous to observe her total lack both of self-acceptance and self-discipline. Predictably, she behaved impulsively, irrationally and emotionally. She was a most attractive young adult, but unable to sustain a relationship with even one of the many persons unlucky enough to have been significant in her life... including myself. One day, in great frustration, I confronted her, "How can you expect to sustain any happiness in life if you insist upon violating every rational rule in this world?" She paused, the silence poignant, before she asked, "What rules of the world? Tell me what they are, I never heard of them." "Believe me," I fervently agreed, "You've got a deal. I'll be ready for you tomorrow!" And I was. Thus were born my "Rational Rules of the World."

Over the years I have amended these 'Rules' a bit, but they have stood the test of time pretty much as they were originally generated. That young woman and her cooperative parents stuck like glue to those 'Rules' and she began to mature, at last, a feat which several hospital programs had been unable to accomplish. They work. Since that day many former clients have copied my 'Rational Rules of the World' to share with their mates and teach their children. The 'Rules' summarize succinctly every principle presented in this book, designed to help your child in 'growing up good.'

RATIONAL RULES OF THE WORLD

1. THE WORLD IS NOT ALWAYS FAIR.
2. EVERYBODY HAS A BOSS SOMETIMES.
3. YOU CAN STAND 'AWFUL' LONG ENOUGH TO MAKE A GOOD PLAN.
4. LIVING INVOLVES HASSLE, EVERY SINGLE DAY.
5. TRUE PRIDE IS SELF-RESPECT AND MUST BE EARNED, NOT GIFTED.
6. YOU CAN DO HARD THINGS... YOU ARE NOT A POPSICLE OR A NOODLE.
7. WHAT YOU DO MATTERS... BUT YOU ARE NOT WHAT YOU DO.
8. EVERYBODY GOOFS, A LOT. PRACTICE LAUGHING AT YOUR GOOFY MISTAKES.
9. NOBODY IS ENTITLED TO ANYTHING... NO ONE MUST DO WHAT YOU COMMAND.
10. BEING LOVED IS FREE ONLY FOR BABIES... AFTER THAT YOU HAD BETTER GIVE TO GET.
11. YOU ARE NOT A PUPPET. YOU HAVE THE POWER TO CHOOSE HOW YOU THINK, HOW YOU FEEL AND HOW YOU ACT.
12. STAYING HAPPY INVOLVES EFFORT AND ACTION.

Hang this chart of the RATIONAL RULES OF THE WORLD in a prominent place at home and attend to it with the same diligence accorded those ABC charts found in every primary classroom. Remember, this fourth 'R' merits equal status! For a time, you must be the one to discover and identify any Rational Rule that pertains to your child's behavior choices. Gradually, however, you can designate Alex and Ashley as 'detectives,' guiding them to search for the appropriate, relevant rule. Each time, with kindness and humor, review the 'Rule' and engage your child actively in the discussion and problem resolution.

Character develops slowly, over time. A personal philosophy of life and how one relates to himself and others takes so much more time, so much more effort than acquiring those classic three 'R's. Teachers, religious leaders, coaches, friends, personal experiences and, yes, genetics, all contribute to how your unique angel develops. But you, the parent, can be the most powerful influence of all.

Perhaps this book can best end how it began, by restating from the Introduction...

> *... to me, 'growin' up good' means a child grows gradually and steadily in his ability to own responsibility for himself; how he thinks, how he feels and how he acts. An adult person who has 'grown up good' understands that he is not perfect and that no one else is either. So he doesn't take himself too seriously and can laugh at the absurdities of our 'humanness.' That makes*

him an understanding, forgiving and loving person. He pursues his wants in life with gusto, without collapse when he runs into those inevitable hassles and when they occur, he can discipline his disappointments and move on, reasonably. That makes him the captain of his emotional ship, not its victim. A child who is 'growin' up good' feels happy in a contented, peaceful way most of the time and he has developed a set of values which reasonable people admire. You will like your child, others will like him and most important he will like himself. What else would you really want for your child?

Addendum

ENTRENCHED ENTITLEMENT: DECLARE WAR!

... "All is fair in love and war."

In Chapter E we discussed how an entire family becomes dysfunctional when just one member proves to be an Entrenched GIMMEE-PIG, because every element of the FAMILY FARE principles becomes habitually violated. That is, the Entitled Royal I'Ness gives himself permission to behave UNSAFELY and UNFAIRLY, following none but his own dictates. His words and tone are often unkind, attacking and disrespectful, with the results no fun for anyone!

If your FAMILY FARE has been invaded seriously enough and long enough for you to feel despair, you might need to consider Alex or Ashley's Entitlement as a developmental disorder, a condition that requires strong remediation. Think of it this way. If your child became malnourished you would understand that you could not treat that condition incidentally, with merely an overnight remedy. You would need an aggressive treatment regimen over a sustained period. So, too, with Entrenched Entitlement, a condition that was allowed to develop firmly and which cannot be eradicated with only a casual confrontation. Entrenched Entitlement is like a house overrun with cockroaches. The damage is everywhere and nothing will suffice, short of all-out WAR.

Just in case the message is not clear, let me say it another way. If you have granted you child overspecialing and adult status prematurely, you have made a giant miscalculation. You have let a poisonous vapor out of a bottle that spreads across the entire homefront. What a dilemma! What to do? Ignoring the problem is definitely not the solution, but how do you recapture the noxious fumes? With difficulty, I am sorry to report. But take heart! It can be done.

If your child is an adolescent with Entrenched Entitlement you may well need some professional help, since you are suffering a double whammy! Even normal adolescents bring a truckload of obnoxious, testing behaviors combining a new surge of dangerous GIMMEEs and I DONWANNAs with unbelievably poor judgment. Almost every adolescent will look and sound like an Entitled Royal I'Ness some of the time, a difficult stage to endure but which will pass, with some good luck and plenty of humor. However, an Entrenched adolescent GIMMEE-PIG is quite something else, and his pattern of behaviors may be beyond your control. You will know the difference because the problem behaviors of entrenchment will show long before adolescence arrives.

When a pre-adolescent Royal I'Ness presents in your home the condition is salvable, but remember, it won't be easy, and you will need to bring out some heavy armamentaria, tantamount to declaring war! You must be willing to take an action quickly and decisively, and to follow through, both on monitoring your child and in carrying our consequences. The main ingredient will be action, not explanation. Recall Chapter B, and remember the AINs. Be prepared to have your child enraged at you, while you remain unimpressed. Even under attack you must remain calm and respectful, without losing your cool. This is imperative, because if you sound 'mean-spirited' your cunning GIMMEE-PIG will switch confrontation away from his entitlement behavior onto an attack upon you for 'acting so mean.' To a child of Entitlement, any hint of anger expressed toward him merely results in his self-granted permission to exonerate himself from his misbehavior, thus 'reinforcing' his own unreasonable concept of fairness. While he has little or no sensitivity to the rights of others, he is finely tuned to his own feelings of outrage and humiliation, and this self-concern supersedes the original confrontation, from his perspective.

Take an inventory of your internal fortitude. Are you prepared to wage an all out war to rescue your child? Do not start a half-baked war, because you will not succeed. An entrenched Royal I'Ness will overpower you, outmaneuver you, outlast you, with his strong but outrageous personage. Think carefully. If you are not ready to be gutsy, don't start the program. Go back and suffer more victimization until you have finally endured enough! Then, and only then, study the following strategies, roll up your sleeves, and declare WAR. The siege will end after a few months if you persevere relentlessly.

STEP ONE: Announce to your Entitled Royal I'Ness that for at least the next few months, there will be new rules in the home. Starting tomorrow, you and your child will be playing a game called WAR. Your child will be put on rations for all privileges and luxuries and special services, specifically all GIMMEEs and IDONWANNAs. Alex and Ashley will continue to receive free necessities such as air, regular meals, basic clothing and all small essentials like milk money and carpool rides to school. Because they are 'lucky' they will also be given a little free positive attention, encouragement, and nursing care. However, the general rule is NOTHING IN YOUR FAMILY LIFE WILL BE FREE for now. Nothing! Explain carefully that WAR is not declared against him, but that all of you, together, need to declare WAR on his Entitlement. When will the war game end? Whenever this dreadful problem called ENTITLEMENT goes away and stays away for at least a month, with no visible symptoms remaining.

STEP TWO: Precisely define the kinds of behavior that qualify as ENTITLEMENT to you. Use the following 10 categories which you are to list on a chart and post in a conspicuous, convenient place. This chart will help Alex and Ashley to be aware of what they are doing.

HAPPY MOUTH . . .
This means your child must remain pleasant, without name-calling, muttering, demanding, complaining, arguing, criticizing, teasing, etc. For example, if your child says, "I hate you! You are a mean mother!," you say, "I do not talk to you like that and you may not to me. You must go someplace else, alone, to talk ugly."

OBEYING . . .
This means you will insist that your child obeys you every time you make a request for action, such as "come here," "please start your bath," "turn off the TV," no matter if he disagrees or dislikes your tone. Your child simply must obey

you, in the final showdown. To allow him to refuse an edict is truly a disservice to him because he then feels empowered to ignore the 'rules of the world,' to believe he is entitled to special exemptions from social expectations.

GOOD LISTENING . . .
This means your child communicates to you that he has heard your call or request. Ignoring you or choosing to remain silent when you call him is absolutely not acceptable. If he does not process well, he needs to not only answer you, but restate your message in his own words, so you know he 'got the message.'

ACCEPTING LIMITS . . .
This means your child will refrain from any 'lawyering' behavior... bargaining, pleading, cajoling, negotiating, threatening. This includes no GIMMEE-PIGGING, in which, if given an inch, he immediately goes for two. This also includes accepting "NO" from you in response to a request, and remembering not to act without permission.

PLAYING FAIR . . .
This means not only the obvious good sportsmanship required in playing games, such as taking turns and not cheating, but the much larger concept of recognizing the rights of others. Remember, the Entitled child defines 'fairness' incorrectly. When you observe an abuse, say, "You are not playing fair. Other people have rights and you must honor them. Everyone counts equally."

TEMPER CONTROL . . .
This means all aggressive behaviors that cause pain, destruction or rudeness, such as hitting, kicking, biting thrashing, tantruming, slamming doors, stamping, destroying walls, furniture etc. If your child trashes his room in a rage, he must put it back in order before gaining exit. If there is real destruction, he must play a part in paying and helping with

the mending. If he has no money saved, sell his bicycle or favorite toy to help pay. It is important that he understands you mean business.

MAGIC WORDS (APPRECIATION) . . .
This refers specifically to the magic words of 'please,' 'thank you' and 'may I?' The magic words are not only necessary, but so is an appropriate tone, conveying sincerity. If offered one cookie, he may not ask for two, nor respond with anger, disdain or disappointment when he is not allowed to be GIMMEE-PIGGISH.

KINDNESS . . .
This means your child can be expected to be helpful to another, even if such is not his job, nor is required. If you can observe him offering kindness without expecting immediate reciprocity, especially if the kindness involves sacrifice or inconvenience, praise him and acknowledge the deed. Say, "I really appreciated your kindness. You were a true friend and true friends are very valuable."

UNCLE! (YIELDING) . . .
This means that difficult skill of accepting defeat, of yielding at least politely or quietly, if not graciously, when events do not go his way. Entitled children have little or no tolerance for frustration or perceived humiliation. They often view every request as a power struggle, every refusal or loss as an insult or 'put down.'

TOGETHERNESS (COOPERATION) . . .
This means those family times when your Entitled child needs to cooperate with a brother or sister without dissension and without parental involvement for a specific period of time. This might include homework time, dinner time, riding in an auto, visiting a relative, sharing a game, staying with a sitter. The time period has a definite start and finish.

Everyone of these 10 categories involves social interaction. Please note that this chart does not focus upon rewarding responsible behaviors such as making a bed, or brushing teeth, so commonly used in popular behavior-modification contracts. Training a child to act responsibly is always a worthy goal, of course, but this program called WAR is designed to focus specifically upon the main ingredient of Entitlement, basically a social problem between your Royal I'Ness and other humans, a problem between your Royal I'Ness and his unrealistic expectations, including his warped perception of fairness.

STEP THREE: Explain the game. Each morning when Alex (or Ashley) wakes up, he is to be given 10 poker chips (or tokens of some kind) absolutely free, which he will need for purchasing all his GIMMEEs and IDONWANNAs. The purpose of the WAR game is for Alex to avoid 'STEPPING ON A MINE' which he will do every time he goofs in one of the categories listed on the chart. When he steps on a mine, Alex must yield a token, immediately, on-the-spot. Now this is not a good way for him to waste his chips, because he will need them for his pleasures... but choosing to waste chips or not must always be his decision.

The power of the program depends upon immediate feedback and payment action, with no delay. Therefore, in the WAR game, parents do not need to do elaborate bookkeeping or charting of what Alex earns or spends on a daily basis, although you may wish to do so. You do not delay accountability across an entire week, a standard procedure in most behavior modification programs. Neither does Alex 'earn' for positive behaviors, another common tenet in most programs. You simply collect a token at the moment of the goof, simultaneously commiserating with Alex when he has 'stepped on a mine.' There are many varieties of reward/cost programs, but for a child of Entitlement I have found that requiring him to yield a chip immediately upon the misbehavior to be more effective than his earning chips for the absence of goofs. The immediacy of the feedback and the experience of actually handing over a chip seems to be crucial. Also, the entire flavor of the program can be carried out with a positive tone. The GIMMEE-PIG usually loves the idea of being given something for nothing, to start with... it matches his own perception of fairness... and also, it allows you to remain empathetic (but firm!) when he steps on a mine.

The tokens will quickly become important to Alex and Ashley because they are needed to purchase all their GIMMEE luxuries and LEMMEE privileges. If Alex spends too many chips on IDONWANNA behaviors, which is what he is choosing to do every time he 'steps on a mine,' he will suffer from empty pockets later in the day when he needs his chips, to watch a half-hour of TV, or invite over a friend, or enjoy a delicious treat. On the other hand, if he is careful not to 'step on a mine' he will have plenty of chips to enjoy his usual lifestyle, and perhaps even to enjoy extra bounties accorded victorious warriors. Remember the rule: NOTHING IS FREE except essentials! In WAR, martial law is often declared during a critical time, on a temporary basis. So it will be, in your home. Never mind if Alex's bike was a birthday gift, or if he bought his computer game with his own money. All items are to be confiscated during the WAR, to be rationed out only by payment and ONLY on a rental basis, by the one/half hour. Be prepared for your Royal I'Ness to squeal like a true GIMMEE-PIG about some of the rules. Initially,

Alex and Ashley probably will be happy about receiving ten free chips for 'nothing' but their enthusiasm will be short lived when they must actually start to pay up for all their luxuries, privileges and goofs, which they had always considered their free rights. They will scream 'foul' and your ears will tire of hearing, "that's not fair!" They will beg and then command you to abandon "this stupid game!." Put cotton in you ears, if you must, but REMAIN RESOLUTE AND CALM, and do not negotiate. Not infrequently a Royal I'Ness will rip up his chart in an effort to reestablish that HE is in charge and the HE can choose to abolish the program. Such behavior, of course, only underscores the necessity of the program. The important discrimination for your Royal I'Ness to absorb is that, while he may choose to ignore or violate the rules, he cannot abolish the program... at least not for awhile. Later he will be told how he does have the power to end the WAR game, by victory.

Even freedom of speech is somewhat curtailed in WAR and your Entitled child is not to be allowed freely to complain or demand an explanation because to do so is unfair to you. It tires your ears. DO NOT BE FAINT-HEARTED. Persist despite your child's upsettedness. You do not need to get angry, but neither do you need to feel guilty about appearing unfair to your child.

If acting in an autocratic manner is alien and reprehensible to you, talk to yourself. Remind yourself that this WAR is only temporary. Remind yourself that every single child of Entitlement is suffering from an overabundance of 'fairness' which has pervaded his short life and is hurting him... Entitlement is the core of his problem, and it needs remediation. Remind yourself that you will remain fair, as a general principle, even during

WAR, but just not according to HIS definition. He cannot be allowed to determine what is fair. You will. And you will no longer worry about whether he agrees. Eventually, your family will return to a more democratic structure, but not just yet. Wrong time to practice democracy! Remind yourself that being firm does not mean being cruel or rude, and that you need only to stay calm and let the program work for you. Rehearse these internal statements so that you will stay resolute.

Alex and Ashley will be spending their tokens either by purchasing their comforts and fun, or by 'stepping on a mine.' Both forms of spending require immediate payment. Foremost, stepping on a mine means pay-up immediately after the goof. Second, all negotiations require chip-in-hand: no chip means no purchase.

For purchasing fun, the limits are clear. Your child may spend all his 10 chips for the day and still he may continue to have a free but somewhat boring membership in the family, but no more purchases until tomorrow, when he will receive his next 10 free chips, automatically. If Alex goes through the day and has not spent all his chips, he may bank his surplus, in a jar, but chips in the bank have special rules. They may be used ONLY for long term larger pleasures (such as a night out for supper and a movie with Mom and Dad, or inviting a friend to spend the night, or saving for an expensive toy). If you wish, you may build a bonus into your WAR game: any day that goes by, with absolutely no mine explosion, results in a bonus of three extra chips to be placed only in the chip bank, reserved for big-time expenditure, such as a new bike, a vacation trip, a new computer game.

A dilemma may occur. If Alex has spent all his chips for today and he has empty pockets, what happens if he then 'steps on a mine'? Remember: THERE MAY BE NO DEFICIT SPENDING. Banked chips can be used only for big-time luxuries, and are not available for BAIL OUT. So, under this circumstance, Alex loses his family membership for the rest of that day, no matter what time of day the mine exploded. It is a privilege to be a member of a happy family, operating on the principles of FAMILY FARE. Alex cannot maintain his membership for that day, so he goes to his room until tomorrow (no free goodies or fun stored there, please!) No scolding on your part. Just a calm application of the WAR rules. Alex is temporarily a prisoner of war (POW), so to speak. He is confined to his room for the rest of that day or evening. He is always allowed essential basics brought to him and he is accorded dignity, even as a Pow. He is allowed to have his homework and school books with him. He will be bored, but that is an unfortunate consequence for losing his free family membership. He is not given special attention and there cannot be any explaining, comforting or negotiating. It is done. His day ends. That's it. His dues are considered paid in full and the next morning he starts off with his full 10 chips.

STEP FOUR: Observe what GIMMEEs and LEMMEEs your child tends to value most. List them and label them a MENU. The menu will need to include all the privileges, luxuries and services available, each with a price assigned. You child may help to prepare the menu, suggesting items with which you agree. A rule about shopping from this menu at any given time is that your child may request to purchase, but not demand. You are always allowed to refuse a request, even from the acceptable list, if the time is not convenient for you. Remember, you do not owe privileges. On the other hand, parents are not allowed to charge chips arbitrarily, for non-defined mines. Any behavior labeled a 'mine' (along with its price tag) must be well defined, in advance, so that your child has been given ample warning about the behavior and knows what it will cost him should he choose to engage in it. This provides a fairness safeguard for him against arbitrary irritation from a parent. From time to time Alex or Ashley will suggest a new pleasure they may wish to add to the menu which can be priced and added to the list. Most parents have trouble starting a list and affixing prices, so here is a sample of commonly used pleasures and services. You will want to make some adjustments depending upon the age and desires of you own special Royal I'Ness.

SAMPLE MENU		
ITEM	**DESCRIPTION**	**COST**
All activities	TV, computer games, riding bike, playing ball with Dad, etc.	1 chip per half hour
Miscellaneous Items	Toys, extra snacks, tickets, cash, extra clothes and big toys (popular items which may be too expensive to charge fully for the child and will require common sense pricing.)	These each have separate prices according to the desirability or expense of the item. Cash often costs one chip for 10 or 25 cents (depending on the child's age and your budget).

Bigger Privileges	A night out with supper and a movie or having a friend spend the night.	10 chips each
All services provided by Mother of Dad (in order for the child to appreciate services rendered to them).	Driving to the mall, delivering friends, extra laundry service, helping with homework.	1 chip each time
All services which are forced upon a parent due to 'stepping on a mine.'	Special annoying, unfair services* such as MAID service, TAXI service, ESCORT service, POLICE service, TUTORING service.	A minimum of 2 chips each time.

* Examples of:

TAXI Service . . .

Child forgot lunch; Mom delivers it to school.

Child misses school bus; parent must drive.

Child gets into trouble; parent must go retrieve.

MAID Service...

Child did not set table (his job) and Mother does it.

Child did not walk dog; Dad does it.

Child left wet towels, dirty clothes all around; Mom does it.

ESCORT or POLICE Service...

Child refuses to obey, to go to his room, and parent must escort him. If parent must continue to monitor, that is POLICE service.

Child refuses to stay on task doing homework, causing parent to constantly monitor or police.

TUTORING Service...

Child requests homework help but then behaves miserably when parent tries to help.

Two chip service charges are reserved solely for 'stepping on a mine.' Serving a child by engaging in a pleasure activity such as reading a story, playing a game or driving him to the store or helping a needy child with his homework who remains pleasant and appreciative would not qualify for this double charge. These loving services can be offered for one chip or occasionally given free, IN MODERATION, when Alex is having a good day and truly working hard not to step on a mine. Remember, this WAR program is only temporary and it will not hurt your child to be made aware of how many privileges were afforded him, freely and lovingly, in the good old days. Do not feel guilty charging for your services. Unfortunately, some children would never develop a sense of 'appreciation' without this exaggerated training.

This list serves only as a sample. As creative observers you will identify other pleasures that uniquely appeal to your child. Your 'economy' needs to balance in this way: If your child had a 'perfect' day and only occasionally 'stepped on a mine,' how many items on that list would you feel comfortable allowing him to experience in one day? Whatever that is, adjust the cost per item so that the sum of a near perfect day would add up to 10. In that system, a child who is careful not to violate the FAMILY FARE rules would experience a day of abundant pleasures plus a few chips left over to bank for a long-term GIMMEE. Of course a child of Entrenched Entitlement will not come even close to a perfect day, at first, so he will end up having to choose among (or forfeit) some pleasure he had been accustomed to receive abundantly in the past.

STEP FIVE: Introduce Alex and Ashley to some new phrases you will be using in the WAR, all of which describe behaviors unacceptable to you:

MOSQUITO BEHAVIOR . . .
This means your child is annoying you with his pesky, nagging, hovering, attention-seeking maneuvers. These are not horror behaviors, but still you will feel like 'slapping at the mosquito.' Say, "You feel like a mosquito nipping at me. It feels pesky. Stop it NOW."

LAWYERING BEHAVIOR . . .
This means your child is continuing to argue, dialogue, debate, bargain, negotiate, much like a lawyer in court. Say, "stop! We are not in court. No more words."

TIRED EARS . . .
This means you are tired of listening to your child. Particularly when he is tantruming, lawyering or mosquitoing. Say, "Stop! You are tiring my ears, and that is not fair to me. I do not want to listen any more."

WALKING ON MY RIGHTS . . .
"You are walking on my rights." This is what you say every time your child does not play fair with you. Tell him so, even when he is not aware of how he is violating, but you, nonetheless, are being forced to own the problem, (such as driving him to school when he has missed the bus, and it is too far to let him walk; he forgot to walk the dog, a task that cannot be delayed; you are running to his room several times to awaken him, etc.).

GLOOMING . . .
This means your child is resorting to pouting, moping, refusing to talk, muttering, wallowing in self-pity. Glooming is very unpleasant for everyone to endure. Recognize it as just another weapon used by a too-special child to control others. Surely you must know adults who have honed this tool to perfection. It starts in childhood and ruins the development of healthy intimacy. Parents love this term 'glooming' because it helps them to recognize and label this manipulative behavior. Say, "Please go somewhere else to feel sad. You may dwell on sadness, if you want to, but you can't stay here and gloom all over us."

All of these phrases are colorful and concrete, which makes them highly efficient tools for dialoguing with your child. Please note this important rule in the WAR game:

Always warn your child, for free, when you can sense that he is about to step on a mine and give your warning in a positive, helpful manner. This communicates to your child that you are on his side, that you want him to win the WAR game and that the enemy is not you, but his problem of Entitlement. Declaring that your Royal I'Ness has stepped on a mine is intended to convey firmness, with empathy. It is definitely not intended to be a punitive, "I GOTCHA" power play by parents. Giving a free warning is how you help your child to develop awareness of what he is doing, but as always, this step requires common-sense. Do not let your child 'command' you to give a warning. In some cases, such as with a tantrum, a warning is not appropriate, the violation being too far along. Some children will view a free warning as simply an opportunity to violate each time with one 'freebie.' If this occurs, get tougher and eliminate most of the warnings. Under no circumstances should you ever give more than one free warning or you are sinking back into your old habit of 'EXPLAINING' instead of 'TRAINING.' (Review Chapter B)

A related problem often occurs when a sympathetic parent anticipates that his child is fast approaching the dilemma of DEFICIT SPENDING. Many parents will remain firm until their child has only one or no chips left for the day and then become lenient. Be careful not to fall into this trap! Do not own the problem of helping Alex avoid his chip disaster. If you do that, you are sabotaging the power of your WAR program. Please do not bail him out. Let him experience the outcome of his choices. That is the ONLY way that genuine changes in his social immaturity can come about. What Alex or Ashley will be experiencing is that a happy family life, with an abundance of freely given pleasures, is a privilege, not to be taken for granted. He will be provided, perhaps for the first time, with a new perspective in discriminating between privileges and rights. The lesson is a difficult one, and if your Royal I'Ness has a long history of Entrenched Entitlement, he may test your resolve many times. Learning may be slow, but he can learn.

Another dilemma may occur when Alex or Ashley has earned and paid for a pleasure activity such as playing a game with Mom or Dad. Suddenly, during the activity, the child may revert to unacceptable entitlement behavior such as cheating, or verbally abusing the parent. During WAR the most powerful plan is to end the activity immediately with a kind but firm, "Sorry, you didn't play fair. You walked on my rights." If your child is young, less than 9 or 10 years old, you may choose to give one free warning, especially if the misbehavior is impulsive rather than manipulative, but be careful. One warning only... after that, be sure to end the privilege immediately if your child persists in his Entitlement behavior. He forfeits the price of the privilege, of course. No refunds.

Two questions are always raised by parents about to embark upon a WAR program: how long must the WAR last and what about other children in the family?

The WAR must last as long as it takes to bring about some consistently new social awareness and behaviors in your special Royal I'Ness. Some children change rapidly, others balk and test the reality over and over again. How long your child has been allowed to reign in your household, how vulnerable you have been as parents, how quickly, consistently and ably you carry out your new role as Commander General, the age of your child, how serious you consider the problem and how strong the basic nature of your child all are variable factors. Rate of progress will be affected by how successfully you have identified, heightened and controlled important GIs for your child. If, in the middle of your program your Royal I'Ness receives a flood of freebies–(birthday money, Christmas, Chanukah presents) you will experience an immediate setback... beware! Perhaps the most important predictor is whether you can remain humorful and empathetic but very firm. The program can be phased out gradually after your child can go a full month without stepping on any mines. Explain that to your child, so he will understand that he has the power to end the WAR. The WAR game ends not by his tearing up the chart or outmaneuvering you but by his walking through his field of FAMILY FARE without stepping on mines.

About another child in the family. You can choose to involve the other, non-entitled child, or not. Some siblings love the idea of joining the 'game' and ask to participate. If so, let the child join, but you may wish to alter different behaviors, more relevant to that child. Or, you can announce that WAR is declared only as a last resort when a problem has not been resolved by other means, and that just because one child has a problem does not mean that another child needs to take medicine. If you choose not to include the sibling, be sure that sibling does not end up with fewer GIMMEEs, LEMMEEs or free attention than your Royal I'Ness earns. You would not want your other child to conclude that misbehaving pays off. The siblings of an Entitled child need to be carefully considered, because they often pay a big price sharing family membership with a GIMMEE-PIGGY.

In review, here are the nuggets of how to declare WAR

should you decide that your Royal I'Ness suffers from Entrenched Entitlement and needs a structured program:

- Label all behaviors that qualify as 'stepping on a mine.'
- Determine the cost in chips, for each explosion.
- Prepare a list of GIMMEEs, LEMMEEs and services available to be purchased.
- Give your child 10 free chips each morning, to be spent or banked. All banked chips are to be used only for long term special pleasures.
- Remember...there can be NO DEFICIT SPENDING.
- Deficit spending must result in your child completing his day and evening in his room, devoid of hidden goodies. He is a POW.
- All pleasures and services and luxuries must be purchased. Only a few necessities in family living will be free (basics—food, bed, clothes).
- Do not 'help' your child with last minute adjustments to avoid POW status. You are to remain pleasant, humorful and empathetic, but never to bailout your child.
  POW experience will not hurt him, but will actually help him grow up, socially.

- Each day is a fresh start, with 10 more chips, no matter yesterday.
- Fade out the program after one month of almost no exploded mines.

Do not sabotage the WAR program. Let the program do the work. Your child needs to experience that Entitlement behaviors have a predictable and negative effect in real life encounters. There is just no better way for him to grasp this reality if he is an already established 'dyed in the wool, too-precious, Entitled Royal I'Ness GIMMEE-PIG'! If, during the program you determine that you are flailing, take your program to a professional expert for review and guidance. I hope you will believe me and will be a parent loving enough and brave enough to rescue your child from this serious developmental disorder before he becomes an overgrown child masquerading as an adult.... "All is fair in love and war."